ABOUT CEM

The Christian Education Movement is an ecumenical educational charity which works throughout the United Kingdom. Its aims are:

- to support religious education in schools;

- to increase awareness of the spiritual, moral, social and cultural dimensions of the curriculum;

- to articulate Christian perspectives on education.

CEM is committed to the teaching of the major world faiths in religious education, and to an accurate and fair representation of their beliefs, values and practices in all its teaching materials.

CEM fulfils these aims:

- by publishing teaching materials and background papers together with a termly magazine *RE Today* and the *British Journal of Religious Education*;

- by offering professional development and consultancy services through its professional staff;

- by arranging national and regional courses for teachers, pupils and others interested in education;

- by research and curriculum development work;

- by supporting the Professional Council for Religious Education and publishing its journal *Resource*.

CEM is funded primarily by the subscriptions of schools and individuals, who find its services essential to their work, and by the sale of publications and professional development services. It also receives funding from local education authorities, churches and trusts. It is a partnership between all those concerned with the religious, spiritual and moral development of children and young people. It is regularly consulted by The Department for Education and Employment, the Qualifications and Curriculum Authority and Ofsted.

To receive further details of CEM resources and subscription services, send to the address below:

Christian Education Movement, Royal Buildings, Victoria Street, Derby, DE1 1GW, Tel: 01332 296655, Fax: 01332 343253, E-mail: cem@cem.org.uk, Website: http://www.cem.org.uk

First Edition 1991

Revised and Expanded Second Edition 1995

Revised and Expanded Third Edition 2000

ISBN 1–85100–141–7

Cover photographs by courtesy of Christian Aid / Elaine Duigenan

All rights reserved. No part of this book may be reproduced in any form or by any means, including information storage and retrieval systems, without permission in writing from the publisher, except by a reviewer who may quote passages in a review, or by an educational institution which has a license from the Copyright Licensing Agency and is operating within the terms of that license.

C000006258

The Baptist Union of Great Britain

The Church of England

The Church of Scotland

Churches Together in Britain and Ireland

The Methodist Church

The Russian Orthodox Church
in Great Britain and Ireland

The Religious Society of Friends (Quakers)

The Roman Catholic Church

The Salvation Army

The United Reformed Church

What the Churches Say

on moral and social issues

———•———

Revised and Expanded Third Edition

———•———

Published by the Christian Education Movement

in partnership with the Churches

———•———

© *CHRISTIAN EDUCATION MOVEMENT 2000*

———•———

ISBN 1–85100–141–7

Relationships and Family • The Beginning of Life • Gender

Homosexuality • Substance Abuse • The End of Life

Prejudice and Discrimination • Law and Order • Work

Money Matters • Animal Welfare • Bioengineering

Environment and World Development • Peace and War

Contents

About this Publication 3

Why the Churches Speak on Moral and Social Issues 4

How the Churches Decide 6

1 • Relationships and Family 20

2 • The Beginning of Life 28

3 • Gender 37

4 • Homosexuality 41

5 • Substance Abuse 47

6 • The End of Life 51

7 • Prejudice and Discrimination 57

8 • Law and Order 62

9 • Work 68

10 • Money Matters 72

11 • Animal Welfare 77

12 • Bioengineering 80

13 • Environment and World Development 85

14 • Peace and War 92

Useful Addresses and Resources 97

Index 104

About this Publication

The first edition of this publication appeared in 1991 as a response to the needs of upper secondary pupils who are required to know the views of Christians on a range of moral and social issues for examination purposes or as part of their general religious education course. It contained statements from seven major Churches on six broad groups of moral and social issues which were found to be among the most common covered in schools. In the extensively revised and greatly expanded second edition, produced in 1995, the same seven Churches covered eleven areas. In this third edition, not only has the range of issues been widened again (to fourteen) but two more Christian traditions are represented – the Church of Scotland and The Russian Orthodox Church. Statements from ecumenical organisations have also been included for the first time.

Pupils need to appreciate that while certain basic principles have been generally held by the majority of Christians over many centuries, there is constant debate about how these principles should be applied in different circumstances. Thus the sanctity of human life might be recognised as an important principle yet Christians might differ on whether it was right for a badly deformed foetus to be aborted or a doctor to hasten the death of a severely ill patient.

It seemed for these reasons important to offer at the outset statements on *why* the Churches offer judgements on moral and social issues and on *how* they arrive at judgements on these issues, while also clearly indicating the extent to which a variety of viewpoints may exist side by side. The *processes* by which judgements are reached are as important as the conclusions.

Not all the Churches have contributed statements on every issue. It would be quite false to assume, however, that these issues are unimportant for the non-contributing Churches. Indeed it could be that they are seen as so important that a fierce debate is taking place and for this reason it is not possible to produce an agreed statement at this time. A Church may also have decided not to offer a contribution on an issue where its views would merely be repeating those of other Churches in order to have more room to explain in detail its views on an issue where its stance is more distinctive.

It needs to be borne in mind that the average length of each Church's entry on any one issue is only 300 words. Many of those who have been responsible for writing these entries have pointed out that this a serious limitation when trying to deal adequately with issues which are often complex and controversial. In many cases these entries are summaries of very substantial reports and we would encourage schools to obtain a copy of these longer documents wherever possible.

Because this book contains basic information which a teacher might use with a variety of groups at a variety of levels, no attempt has been made to tailor it directly to the needs of a particular group of pupils. It is for individual teachers to decide in what form and at what level to present this material to their students.

If it is considered appropriate to present pupils with a copy of some part of the text, photocopying for this purpose is permitted within any institution which has purchased the book, has a license from the Copyright Licensing Agency and is operating within the terms of that license. Copyright remains with CEM however, and photocopying of the entire publication is not permitted.

Why the Churches Speak on Moral and Social Issues

Throughout this publication the word 'Church' is used for convenience to include organisations like The Religious Society of Friends (Quakers) and The Salvation Army who do not normally use it to describe themselves. Where 'church' is used (without a capital letter), it means a local congregation.

All Christians agree that their religion is not just a personal matter. The Gospel makes moral demands which have implications for social activities and public life as well as for personal morality. The Christian Churches therefore have a number of reasons for wanting to be involved in moral and social matters.

1 Christian belief and experience

This is God's world

All Christians, whatever their views on the way in which the universe began, believe that it is God's creation. All that exists is the result of God's activity. He is the Creator, Father and Sustainer of everything and is concerned with every part of our lives. It matters to God how people behave in themselves, how they treat one another and how they use the resources of the universe. The best way to behave morally and socially is to act in harmony with God's intentions. This view is shared by all theistic religions.

God's concern is focused in Jesus

For Christians a major reason for social and moral concern is their belief that in Jesus they see God at work in his world. Jesus expressed God's attitude to the social and moral issues of his time. His followers, therefore, have to try to express God's attitude to the social and moral issues of their own time.

We have a tradition to follow

Before the time of Jesus the prophets declared that God required people to show justice and compassion. Since the time of Jesus the Church, through its saints, leaders and councils, has provided guidance on how the demands of the Christian Gospel are to be applied to all the opportunities and problems which human beings and human societies face.

2 The need for continual discussion and clarification

The complexity of modern issues

Though all Christians take the Gospel to be the foundation of their faith, the human language in which it is expressed is always imperfect and its application to particular circumstances is a matter of judgement. Through the advances of technology and the deepening of knowledge our understanding of life is based on different assumptions from those held in the times of Moses or Jesus. Throughout history, therefore, the Churches have found it necessary to define, or redefine, the application of Christian moral standards to new issues opened up by advances in science, or to old issues in the light of new knowledge. On some issues the Churches have spoken with a single voice but on others Christians have disagreed.

The search for agreement

Although there are still disagreements or differences of emphasis on many moral and social issues between the different Churches, often the areas of agreement and disagreement cut across Church boundaries. Teachers should therefore be wary of suggesting that *all* Christians or even *all members of a particular Church* agree on a particular moral stance. Today, although differences still exist, there is a growing willingness to co-operate in the study of their attitudes to social and moral issues, and to understand each others' beliefs which are the basis for these attitudes. In this way the Churches are beginning to speak together with a common voice on social and moral issues wherever possible. Furthermore, the existence of the World Council of Churches and the growth of co-operation between the Churches in Europe means that the Churches of the United Kingdom are beginning to look at such issues in a wider perspective.

3 Education for moral and social thinking and action

Learning the language of moral discussion

One of the problems the Churches encounter when they start to talk about moral issues is the use of the same word to mean different things. For example, Churches use the word *authority* in different ways. Confusion occurs in the use of this word whether it is applied to individuals (ordained clergy or ministers), or to meetings (synods or committees), or to scriptures (the whole Bible or the New Testament) or to various categories of official pronouncements. What does it mean when a particular Church or a particular individual claims that one of these sources is *authoritative*? Dialogue between Christians is only just beginning to unravel the way in which different groups use particular words and thus to reduce the confusion both within and outside the Churches. Clarifying and refining the language of moral dialogue becomes crucial when addressing fundamental questions such as the *absoluteness* of Christian moral standards, that is, the distinction between what is *always* right or wrong and what *may* be right or wrong according to changes in circumstances or to new insights.

Developing moral processes

There are also differences in the methods and processes by which Churches or Christian individuals develop moral attitudes and practices. For some the emphasis is on clear and absolute rules, and the only difficulty is in applying them. For others the emphasis is on individuals or groups coming to their own decisions, and the important thing is how they set about that process rather than the conclusions they reach. This is why some Churches will emphasise the importance of individuals developing and applying moral insights in the light of Christian principles while others will put a greater emphasis on loyalty to an authoritative moral code, or to the Church or congregation of which people are members.

Christian development and Christian ethos

The two approaches outlined in the paragraph above may, in fact, be held in a creative tension. On the one hand it is desirable to nurture the development of individual Christians as independent moral thinkers. On the other hand it is necessary to preserve a Christian way of looking at moral issues as one of the means by which the Church can be distinguished as a body of people. The Churches are therefore also concerned with social and moral issues in order to encourage the religious development of their members and to help them maintain a Christian witness.

How the Churches Decide

Introduction

There are many books which claim to state *what* the Churches think about moral and social issues, though few of them do justice to the variety of viewpoints to be found within the Churches. Even fewer give any indication of *how* the Churches arrive at these views. This section is intended to reveal *the process* of decision-making that occurs in some of the main branches of the Church in Britain.

Reading through the separate contributions it is easy to see certain common strands. All the Churches use a consultative method of arriving at decisions which means that, in principle, the views of every member of the Church can be heard, though final decisions are inevitably made by a representative body of some kind. All the Churches appeal to scripture, tradition and reason as sources of moral values, though they may vary in the emphasis which they place on each of these. This means that they all take notice of biblical insights but they interpret these in the light of how Christians have traditionally understood them, while also allowing for the possibility of new insights gained from recent advances in human knowledge. Finally, and significantly, all the Churches recognise the complexity of many of the moral and social issues which confront us today, and in various ways make allowances for the fact that not all Christians are going to agree about everything.

What unites Christians, therefore, is not that they agree on every issue but that they agree to a considerable extent on how they should go about the process of making moral decisions, and what kinds of argument should carry the most weight.

The headings in the text reflect the situation described above. Each of the Churches was asked to include in its statement something about the role of **scripture**, the **tradition** of the church and the present-day **faith community** in arriving at moral decisions, then to describe the **processes** involved and finally to say how far it was possible for a **diversity of views** to exist within the Church. All the contributing Churches have followed this pattern but it may be thought significant that they do not all deal with them in the same order. For this reason they have been left in the order in which they were submitted and not placed in a standard order for the sake of consistency.

The Baptist Union of Great Britain

Scripture

The basis of the Baptist Union with regard to all matters of faith and practice is stated as follows:

> … that our Lord and Saviour Jesus Christ, God manifest in the flesh, is the sole and absolute authority in all matters pertaining to faith and practice, as revealed in the Holy Scriptures, and that each church has liberty, under the guidance of the Holy Spirit, to interpret and administer his laws.

Scripture, therefore, clearly has a dominant place in determining matters relating to moral and social concern.

Tradition

It has been said that every Baptist church is built on two pillars: evangelism and liberty. For this latter reason, it is not the practice of the Baptist Union to make official statements on behalf of its member churches as this would be restricting the liberty of the individual congregation. This is why the denomination is described as the Baptist Union (of member churches) rather than the Baptist Church.

Faith community

Nevertheless, from time to time specific groups of people within the denomination will issue statements on matters of faith and practice which are approved by the national Annual Assembly. In this sense, therefore, the Assembly becomes the authority or voice of the denomination. At such Annual Assemblies resolutions are passed relating to a variety of issues, which whilst not reflecting the view of every church, would still be regarded as the denomination's considered statement on matters of social and moral concern.

Processes

The process whereby such statements are agreed is as follows. Each local church is a member of a local Association of Baptist churches which approximates in size to that of a County. The Association has its own Council and also an Annual Assembly which acts as a decision-making body. There are twenty-nine Associations grouped together in twelve regional areas. Each local church also sends delegates to the national Annual Assembly, the number depending on the size of its membership. Other bodies, such as Associations and Baptist Colleges also send delegates to the national Assembly. Between Assemblies, action may be taken by the National Baptist Union Council which is composed of representatives of the Associations. In this way every local church can contribute to the statements which are issued by the Annual Assembly. Statements or resolutions are agreed by voting, either by a simple majority or by a proportion of those present and voting.

Diversity of views

Whilst a decision by the national Annual Assembly would be the considered majority view of the denomination, individuals and churches are free to declare their own views on any particular matter. On occasions when the national Annual Assembly has voted on a major matter, individual churches have been given the opportunity to dissociate themselves from the decision.

In addition, individual groups of Baptists and Associations produce their own statements on moral and social issues which may or may not be taken up by the denomination as a whole. They would be presented as a Baptist view or as an individual group's view.

The Church of England

Faith community

For purposes of consultation and administration, England is divided into forty-three dioceses; each diocese is divided into deaneries, each of which consists of several parishes.

The General Synod is the 'parliament' of the Church of England. It contains 560 members and consists of three 'houses' of Bishops, Clergy and Laity, who meet together twice a year.

The House of Bishops consists of all the forty-three diocesan bishops together with nine suffragan bishops elected by their fellow suffragan bishops, totalling fifty-two.

The House of Clergy has about 250 members, most elected by the clergy of their dioceses, together with representatives of the senior clergy.

The House of Laity has about 250 members, eligible for election from the age of eighteen. These are elected by members of Deanery Synods. Each Deanery Synod is composed of representatives of the local Parish Church Councils. Each Parish Church Council is elected by the members of a church who are on the parish register.

Scripture and tradition

Generally the Church of England could be said to derive its authority equally from three sources, like a tripod with three legs, all of which are needed to support the whole.

The first source is scripture, the word of God as revealed in the Bible.

Secondly comes the tradition and practice built up by the experience of Christians worshipping over the centuries.

Thirdly, and equally needed to balance the tripod, comes reasoning. Understanding brought about through modern knowledge helps us in interpreting the scriptures, in caring for the world and its resources and in showing compassion for our fellow human beings in all circumstances.

Processes

The General Synod is unique. It is the only assembly to which Parliament has given power to pass Measures which become English law. The Measures must still be approved by Parliament and go to the monarch for Royal Assent.

In other matters, mainly to do with the work of the clergy, Synod can legislate without needing to secure the approval of Parliament, though they must still have the monarch's approval. Church laws of this kind are called Canons, and are submitted to the monarch through the Home Secretary.

The functions of the General Synod include the following.

1 Central church business

The legislative work covers many areas of church life, including questions of divorce and remarriage. On any matters of legislation, the Synod has to work according to parliamentary procedure. Such legislation must go through at least three stages: general approval of what is proposed after a debate by the whole Synod; revision by a committee to take into account any details the Synod has raised; and final approval by the whole Synod. The final draft of a Measure then goes to the Ecclesiastical Committee of Parliament for checking by parliamentary lawyers. It is formally laid before Parliament, and there is usually a short debate in each House before it goes to the monarch. Most legislation passes through General Synod on simple majority voting, although some matters have to be passed separately in each House by two-thirds majorities of those present and voting.

2 Comment on public issues

The Church has a close interest in public affairs as they affect the physical and spiritual well-being of people in Britain and overseas. Such matters as education, employment, health, justice and the stability of family life, are all of concern to Christians, and the Government takes notice of what the Church of England and the other Churches say in their national synods and assemblies. Debates on such topics can be introduced through a motion from a diocese or a private member, or may be based on well-researched reports produced by one of the specialist departments. When preparing to make statements upon moral issues, the specialist department, or Board, will be asked to produce a theological rationale as guidance in the decision-making process. The most relevant department for moral and social issues is the Board for Social Responsibility. When motions are finally passed, a distinction will often need to be made between a principle laid down by the General Synod and its

practical application, which will need to take account of individual circumstances.

(Material from *Explaining the Church of England*, edited by Margaret Duggan and Robin Bennett, is reproduced by permission of the Central Board of Finance of the Church of England. This series of leaflets has now been replaced by *Introducing the Church of England* – see Useful Addresses and Resources)

The Church of Scotland

Decision making

For the purposes of Church government and decision-making, the Church of Scotland is a hierarchical, conciliar structure. Locally the spiritual affairs of each congregation are administered by its elders sitting as the Kirk Session, which will face day-to-day decisions about the church's local mission and response to difficult situations. In many circumstances, the individual minister has to use his or her discretion, but may turn to elders for advice and guidance. Regionally, the Presbytery initiates some work in the areas of mission, education and so on, and exercises supervision over the congregations in its area. Nationally, the General Assembly, meeting for one week each May, supervises the central work of the church and debates issues of national and international concern, including the most fundamental areas of social and moral interest. Boards and Committees appointed by the Assembly to undertake the ongoing work of the church will bring reports and studies to the whole Assembly to test the mind of the church.

As the national church, the Church of Scotland has an unusual constitutional position, having an independent spiritual jurisdiction protected by an Act of Parliament of 1921. The church tries to behave in ways that are 'in the world but not of it', and never to abuse its independence from some areas of civil law.

Scripture and faith

The Bible is the supreme rule of faith and life, and ministers and elders must subscribe to this assertion. A secondary place is given to the Westminster Confession of Faith, though there are wide areas of liberty of opinion in this respect, and it must be stressed that personal conviction plays a major role in moral teaching and decision-making at local level. This is because the Church of Scotland can normally only give an opinion at a national level if the matter has been the subject of debate and decision-making in the General Assembly or can be clearly deduced from pronouncements of the Assembly in closely related areas of controversy. It can be frustrating for outsiders wanting to know the Church of Scotland's 'position' on an issue to discover that there is no single attitude; but it is the strength of the church that diversity of opinion is treasured amongst those who share common fundamental beliefs in the scriptures and our historical confession.

Ecumenical Organisations

The Council of Churches for Britain and Ireland (CCBI) was established in 1990 to succeed the British Council of Churches. In 1999 its name was changed to Churches Together in Britain and Ireland (CTBI), reflecting what had become the established practice among local groups of churches, which nearly always call themselves 'Churches Together in … ' It co-ordinates the work of its 32 member Churches and liaises with ecumenical bodies in Britain and Ireland. In each of the nations of England, Scotland, Wales and Ireland there are National Ecumenical Instruments which co-ordinate and facilitate the work of the churches in the nation; Churches Together in England (CTE), Action of Churches Together in Scotland (ACTS), Churches Together in Wales (CYTUN) and the Irish ecumenical bodies.

CTBI's structure consists of a Steering Committee which acts as the management group and meets four times a year. The Steering Committee is elected from the Church Representatives Meeting and from the Assembly. The Church Representatives Meeting consists of senior Church officials from all of the member Churches. It meets twice a year to carry forward the ecumenical vision and set the general policy direction for CTBI. Every two years there is an Assembly, which is a larger and more representative group of people from the Churches, networks, and Bodies in Association. It provides a broader testing ground for ecumenical advance and direction and is an important opportunity for people to gather and exchange news and views throughout the four nations and two jurisdictions (United Kingdom and Republic of Ireland) covered by CTBI.

Public statements that the Churches wish to make together through CTBI are made by the Church Representatives Meeting or the Assembly. It is rare for such statements to be made unless a number of member Churches and bodies have already begun to develop their own judgements and request ecumenical co-operation through CTBI to try and reach consensus. In the case of an urgent reaction to a current event, the Presidents or the General Secretary may speak on behalf of the Council subject to consultation with the Steering Committee or the Moderator of the Steering Committee.

Churches Together in Britain and Ireland exists to co-ordinate and facilitate the work of the churches at the four-nation level. At a time of changing political realities, of devolution and regional assemblies, the need for co-ordination between the nations remains essential. The basic principle of the ecumenical instruments is that the Churches are the carriers and promoters of the ecumenical vision. Ecumenism is the project of the Churches and not the ecumenical bodies. The instruments are there to fulfil the Churches' calling to seek visible unity between them.

The Methodist Church

Morality, or ethics, by which we mean 'what is right', is concerned with three types of conduct.

1 Personal

Personal morality is concerned with how people behave *as individuals* towards other individuals, towards the groups to which they belong and towards the world in which they live and its resources.

2 Social

Social morality is concerned with how *groups* behave and how people behave *in groups*. Examples include families, neighbourhoods, football crowds, schools and colleges, workplaces, nations.

3 Public

Public ethics is concerned with what is expected from us and what we properly owe *as citizens* to public organisations. These range from bodies such as local, regional and national government (not forgetting the international or supranational bodies which are increasingly influential in our lives, such as the European Union and the United Nations) to the professional and other bodies such as trades unions, the judiciary, the civil service, the medical profession and so on which play such an important role at a level between the citizen and government.

Scripture and tradition

The basic legal documents of the Church go back to the eighteenth century but are now contained in the *Model Deed* and the *Methodist Church Act* of 1976. These state that the Methodist Church draws its teaching about matters of faith and practice (its doctrinal standards) from two sources

1 The Christian Scriptures

The doctrinal standards of the Methodist Church are 'based upon the Divine revelation recorded in the Holy Scriptures', which revelation Methodism 'acknowledges as the supreme rule of faith and practice'.

2 The Christian tradition

Tradition means teaching (which includes example as well as precept) handed down from one generation to the next. For Methodists this teaching includes 'the Apostolic Faith' and certain writings of John Wesley, the leader of the revival and renewal movement within the Church of England in the 18th century which became the Methodist Church. 'The Apostolic Faith' means the beliefs of the early followers of Christ, as these are expressed in the 'fundamental principles of the historic creeds' (the Apostles' Creed and the Nicene Creed), 'and of the Protestant Reformation'. While John Wesley's writings are respected, neither these nor his brother's hymns are 'intended to impose a system of formal or speculative theology on Methodist preachers'. They serve, rather, as standards which should 'secure loyalty to the fundamental truths of the Gospel of Redemption and ensure the continued witness of the Church to the realities of the Christian experience of salvation'. (*The Deed of Union*, clause 4)

Faith community

These words from *The Deed of Union* highlight the importance of Christian experience in Methodism. In Methodist teaching 'experience' includes emotions, but much else besides: it is the reflective response of all aspects of our being (intellectual, moral, emotional and spiritual) to the person and activity of God in our lives and in creation as a whole. Experience in this broad sense may be mediated through science, art or politics and by other people (who will not necessarily be Christian); and it includes our sense of vocation, our inner values and ambitions, and our discernment of meaning and purpose for our lives.

Christian judgements about personal, social and public ethics are formed as we reflect on the sources of Christian belief and practice in the light of our daily experience of the modern world. As experience changes, our insights, convictions and moral perspectives may grow and develop, or may require to be formulated in new ways.

It is at this point that the faith community of the Church becomes very important, for this experience must of course be tested against the 'fundamental doctrines' of the Christian scriptures and tradition. It is in Church life as a whole, congregational, national and international, that this process of testing takes place. In this way 'the mind of the Church' emerges as to where God is leading us about personal, social and public conduct *for our age*. This whole approach to Christian decision-making in the field of personal, social and public ethics is well illustrated by two paragraphs in the introduction to the 1992 Declaration of the Methodist Conference on *A Christian Understanding of Family Life, the Single Person and Marriage*:

1.21 Everyone – including Christians – who would understand the issues raised by contemporary life must make positive use of the best informed teaching of modern knowledge. In reaching a specifically Christian judgement however, there are three major resources to be brought to bear on the situation and 'the best informed teaching of modern knowledge' upon it: the Christian scriptures; what is taught by the Christian tradition and community; and the personal experience and prayer of Christians.

1.24 The Holy Spirit in the community of the Church is the source of discernment and renewal who enables us to uncover, through a process of spiritual education, and on the basis of well informed modern knowledge what is true and right for today.

Processes

The governing body of the Methodist Church is its annual Conference. Operating within guidelines set out above, the Conference is the formal authority on all matters of belief and practice. Proposals for a change or development of Methodist teaching about personal, social or public Christian ethics can be initiated:

1 by any two representatives to the annual Conference proposing a resolution (known as a Notice of Motion) at the Conference itself;

2 by local groupings of churches (gathered in what are known as Circuit Meetings) or by regional groupings of churches (gathered in a District Synod) proposing a resolution to the Conference;

3 by a resolution to Conference from the Methodist Council (a smaller representative body which meets four times a year between Conferences).

If, by methods 1 and 2 above, the proposed change or development is significant, the Conference will usually direct the Methodist Council to look into the issues and to present a report at a subsequent Conference.

In the course of preparing the report, staff who are appointed or employed by the Council will be responsible for developing the Church's thinking with the help of professional and theological expertise; and must undertake a wide range of consultations – in the Methodist Church itself, with partner Churches (Methodist and ecumenical) in Britain, and elsewhere in the world. Then the report, with or without specific recommendations, will be presented to Conference for debate.

Examples of issues dealt with in this way are: abortion; civil disobedience; nuclear deterrence; the manufacture and sale of arms; disarmament; care of the environment; family and divorce law; gambling; housing; overseas development and fair trading; poverty; racial justice; asylum and immigration issues; human sexuality; political responsibility.

Sometimes the Conference will attempt a definitive judgement on an important theme which is intended to represent the Church's mind for a decade or more. In such cases a final decision is made after two debates in Conference, separated by at least a year, to allow for discussion in all parts of the Church's life. Topics of personal, social or public Christian ethics dealt with in this way become official **Statements** or **Declarations** of the Church on the subject concerned, for example, *Family Life, the Single Person and Marriage*.

Debates in the annual Conference take place in a setting of worship, prayer and bible study, and with prayers for the guidance of God through the presence of the Spirit.

The Russian Orthodox Church

The Orthodox Church founded by the Apostles remains faithful to its Holy Tradition. It maintains an air of antiquity and retains an apparently unchanging character. This given expression of its continuity with the Church of ancient times is reflected in its every expression. 'We do not change the everlasting boundaries which our fathers have set,' wrote John of Damascus (645–750), 'but we keep the Tradition, just as we received it.'

Likewise, the Eastern Patriarchs in the letter of 1718 addressed to Non-Jurors in England said: 'We preserve the Doctrines of the Lord uncorrupted and firmly adhere to the Faith He delivered to us and keep it free from blemish and diminution as a Royal Treasure, a monument of great price, neither adding anything, nor taking anything from it.'

Tradition led to the formation of the Canon of the Scripture, which added to the books of the Old Testament inspired works belonging to the first years of the Church, not determined at one point in time, but put together during the first three centuries. The books of scripture, which were most widely read and acclaimed, became the Christian Bible, and complimenting this was the awareness of the rich oral teachings of Jesus, those not recorded in writings by His immediate disciples.

Challenges of history and heresy led to the convening of councils which were later acclaimed as Ecumenical and Authoritative. The first two of these finalised the Creed in Nicaea (325) and Constantinople (381). The writings of the Fathers established doctrine, the Councils affirmed it. Canons were also formulated so that the whole system of doctrine, church government, worship, spiritual teaching and art were articulated through the ages.

Hence, Orthodox Christians see themselves as heirs and guardians of a rich inheritance of Christian Tradition 'the faith and practice which Jesus Christ imparted to the Apostles, and which since the Apostles' time has been handed down from generation to generation in the Church.' (1Corinthians 15:3).

Scripture

The supreme expression of God's revelation to the human race is the Lord Jesus Christ. The Gospels are the inspired record of this; the Acts of the Apostles and Epistles are a record of the Spirit-filled church. Within this Spirit-filled body of the Church, scripture lives and truly reflects Christ. The Bible is the Book of the Church, but Christians are not people of 'The Book'. It is because the Living Lord Jesus Christ is ever present, alive and active in His Church through the Holy Spirit that scripture has authority.

It is from the Church that the Bible derives its authority (and not the other way round). Only within the Church and in accord with Christian tradition can Holy Scripture be interpreted with authority. Individual Christians must never trust their own personal judgement alone but, by being taught to understand scripture in accordance with the above principles and integrating the teachings of scripture within their own understanding, they are able to make decisions which are appropriate to them.

Faith community

The formulation of key Orthodox doctrine was affirmed in the seven Ecumenical Councils, the last being held in AD 787. In that early period and since then, there have been local councils not claiming to represent the Orthodox Catholic Church as a whole, and letters and statements put out by individual bishops. When these are accepted by the rest of the Church they acquire ecumenical authority. The Ecumenical Councils also drew up canons dealing with church organisation and discipline and there have been other canons made by local councils and individual bishops. There are collected in the Pedalion, the standard Commentary on canon law, (*The Rudder* published in 1800 by Nichodemus of the Holy Mountain). Canons deal with the earthly life of the Church where conditions are constantly changing and individual situations are infinitely various.

In day to day life, there is little reference to these canons but they are understood and accepted within the living tradition and Orthodox Christians follow them, and these rules, governing all aspects of Christian behaviour, are known by all members of the Church, not only bishop and priests, and hence each Christian is equipped for right behaviour shaped by ethical principles and moral and social considerations.

The Bishop is the focus of unity and truth with whom every Christian must be in communion. The bishop, his priests and laity together, in whatever place, possess the wholeness and fullness of church life when they are in communion with the whole Church.

There can be differences of interpretation and advice but these must never be in conflict with Holy Tradition. On primary matters there will usually be general agreement, but on secondary matters there may be diversity of views. Individuals need to grow in the freedom of spiritual awareness in which they can take all these factors into consideration and weigh each one carefully before coming to their own individual decision.

A pastoral approach

A modern writer, Oliver Clement, summarises: 'In a world afflicted by a huge verbal inflation, our ethical reflection must grow out of peace, silence, prayer, and a great hunger for modesty. People discover moral standards through sharing the life of a community, which has inner light, a sense of beauty, and unity in diversity, rather than through lists of taboos proclaimed in a triumphalist and authoritarian atmosphere. Ethical teaching must not be a clerical monologue, a list of things allowed and forbidden. People need to discover the meaning of life, they must be encouraged to change the way they live through the discovery of beauty.' (adapted from Taizé, *un sens a la vie*)

Orthodox Christians should in all things think carefully and pray diligently and consult with a spiritual father or mother. A bishop or priest will stand with them to enable them to determine the will of God and the working of Holy Spirit within them. The priest stands as the minister of the Gospel of Love and never as a judge. Any guidelines, therefore, which the Church might provide, remain in a state of dormancy until brought to life in prayer activated by the Holy Spirit. They have no meaning outside this context, the Christian dynamic. They are seeds of truth lying dormant until watered and nurtured in the life of God.

Great emphasis is paid to the pastoral care of each person who must be in regular contact with a spiritual father or mother. In advice given, a distinction must be made between that of the ethos of the Old Testament and that of the New Testament. We are not children of 'the Book' alone, but disciples of the Living Lord. The Old Testament, understood entirely in the light of the new meaning given by Christ, offers guidance by Law as exemplified in the Ten Commandments, but summarised by Our Lord as 'Love the Lord Thy God with all thy heart, soul, strength and mind and thy neighbour as thyself' (Matthew 22:37–39; Mark 12:30–31). The New Testament offers no such commandments but rather gives The Beatitudes as markers of an exemplary life. Our Lord, above all, gave the example of a God of Love who loves and shows mercy.

Hence, the principle of economy (oikonomia) may be applied but must be understood. It is a pastoral function permitting what may appear to be a relaxation of the letter of canon law, or the practice of the Tradition without violating the spirit of either. It is always used in a particular case without creating precedent and with the intention of furthering God's plan of Salvation. Thus, Patriarch Nicholas Mysticos (901–907, 912–925) said of oikonomia, it is ' … an imitation of God's love for man' and not simply an exception to the rule.

Nicon Patrinacos (in his work *A Dictionary of Greek Orthodoxy*) states that: oikonomia is an acceptable deviation from an established rule for the sake of bringing salvation. In his view, the deviation should not extend to the point where it violates the rule in question but it should be an expression of the love that guides the Church. Such love and compassion is motivated by sympathy, leniency and an understanding of human weakness. This is supported by the guidance of the Fathers. Eulogius, Patriarch of Alexandria (581–607) wrote: 'One rightly can practise oikonomia whenever pious doctrine remains unharmed. Hence oikonomia concerns the practical implications of Christian belief, but it never compromises the Truth itself.' It permits various possible ways of implementing the Christian Gospel in a practical

way. This may lead to a situation where tension and disagreement are unavoidable.

In summary, there are rules and guidelines for all aspects of life in the Orthodox Church but these are applied with pastoral concern to enable individuals and communities to move forward on their spiritual journey. The Church stresses a code of practice which must give support rather than be a crippling constraint. We have a Holy and Sacred Tradition which addresses the whole and every aspect of life, but above all, we honour each and all (every single person and each group of persons) as a Temple of the Holy Spirit. For each is made in the image of God, and at baptism the likeness of God begins to be restored. A holy life means that this image is transformed into a likeness and a real process of deification is under way. Even the greatest sinners, when they show forth an act of love, reveal at that moment in time the supreme God reflected in them, and that revelation urges us to bow down and worship in awe.

Conclusion

For the many reasons described, Orthodox Christians are reluctant and ill at ease with written contributions to an anthology of moral and social issues lest by too much analysis there is a fragmentation of total belief. When subject to categorisation and analysis, we fall into an approach to the Christian life which is totally alien to Orthodoxy. Rather, we prefer to draw on the teachings of the Fathers and make general statements of principle which do have an absoluteness to them, but which nonetheless are for guidance only. They enshrine the truth which is absolute, but they must be interpreted and applied through reflection and prayer, and with the help with an experienced spiritual guide who may enable individuals and couples to find direction and meaning.

In our contribution to this edition, we shall emphasise the importance of Ecology and judicious care of the Environment, for it is only in the perspective of men and women living in harmony with God and His Creation that moral and social issues can be set in a proper context. Only when men and women are united to God, growing into His likeness and seeking to know His will can right moral decisions be made. In separation, human dilemmas may seem insuperable and the best decisions, even though taken with great integrity, may be quite wrong. For separation is sin and always ends in tragedy. Only in Christ are the forces of evil defeated so that all can be made new. Only in God and his Holy Church can we determine the path through what otherwise is a moral maze of great perplexity.

The Religious Society of Friends (Quakers)

Processes

Quakers have no creeds or rules used as tests of membership or means of conformity, but they do have beliefs and practices in common. The most distinctive and widely shared insight is that 'there is that of God in everyone' and our duty to respond to it. Decision making thus begins with an individual's personal experience of those feelings of love and truth described in the Old Testament as 'the still, small voice of God', or by Quakers as the 'Inner Light'. A tentative decision then moves through testing and double-checking in the Meeting (see under Faith community) to a sense that the will of God has been discerned and the decision is therefore clear.

All business, study, discussions and so on are in a spirit of worship. As all Meetings are for worship, silence will be the characteristic framework, with people listening actively to each other, offering contributions rather than arguing or persuading. Votes, motions, counter-motions or amendments are not used. Quakers try to obtain a sense of the Meeting. This sense is not human consensus, nor absolute unanimity, but the agreement and consent of all present that they have reached clearness, so that they feel they have discerned the will of God.

The clerk will draft a minute, which is revised and agreed in the Meeting at the time. Subsequent Meetings will be guided but not necessarily bound by the minute, assuming that the Spirit continues to lead. Those present may be representatives, who have been prepared by the Meetings that sent them, but they are not delegates mandated to a particular view. The process of reaching clarity may take time, years even. The will of God may be found (uncomfortably) to be what nobody in the Meeting wants.

A question, problem or concern (feeling that God calls to a specific task) may arise in one or more people. Decisions, however, may not be simple, and individuals can be mistaken. Personal matters may be taken privately to a small, informal group of overseers, or to any other wise Quakers and friends. More public matters will be taken to the appropriate Meeting and may be referred further, as needed. Committees and groups may be appointed to prepare reports, or carry out decisions.

Faith community

It is the experience of Quakers that the guidance of the Holy Spirit can be known and followed without the need for a separated, ordained clergy. Members may be appointed to specific tasks for limited periods, according to their gifts and abilities, without discrimination of race, gender, sexual orientation, age or social status. Such tasks include those of elders (responsible for the spiritual life of Meetings), overseers (responsible for pastoral care), clerks (serving administrative needs), treasurers, librarians and so on. 'Friend' is the only title used in the Society.

The organisation of the Society's Meetings in reaching decisions is as follows.

Preparative Meetings (local) are held at least weekly for worship; most pastoral care takes place within Preparative Meetings.

Monthly Meetings combine several Preparative Meetings and are responsible for membership, marriage, property, appointments and other decisions.

General Meetings are consultations (now usually twice a year) between the members of several Monthly Meetings.

Britain Yearly Meeting is the short title of the Yearly Meeting of the Religious Society of Friends (Quakers) in Britain. The name refers both to the organisation and to the national annual meeting which all members of Monthly Meetings are eligible to attend. This Meeting is the final authority among British Quakers, and may speak and act on their behalf.

Meeting for Sufferings is the title (dating from the period of Quaker persecution) of the Executive Committee, which includes up to three representatives from each Monthly Meeting and which may, between Yearly Meeting sessions, speak or act on behalf of Quakers in this country.

Tradition

Quakers do not stress the authority of tradition but do have regard to the insights of their past, and especially to those particularly challenging ones they call 'Testimonies'. They look to the many journals, biographies, letters, essays and devotional writings of past and contemporary Friends to learn how others have reached decisions. The most definitive up-to-date guide to Quakerism in Britain is *Quaker Faith and Practice*, subtitled *The book of Christian discipline of the Yearly Meeting of the Religious Society of Friends (Quakers) in Britain*, approved in 1994 and published in 1995. *Quaker Faith and Practice* is revised every generation or so, with every Friend encouraged to contribute. Local Meetings consider drafts, before Yearly Meeting in session agrees to publish. *Advices and Queries* (chapter 1 of *Quaker Faith and Practice*) is widely read in Meetings for worship, and also used in private meditation. They are not rules, but general principles offered as food for thought and meditation, and as challenging questions.

Scripture

Quakers understand the Bible as a record arising from struggles to comprehend God's ways with people. The same Spirit that inspired the writers gives understanding – this is more important than the literal words. While quotations from the Bible may illuminate a truth, Quakers would not use them to prove a truth. The work of scholars in deepening understanding is welcomed.

Diversity of views

Quakerism has Christian roots, and many Quakers would see Christ as the centre of their faith. However, they do not think that revelation stopped when the Bible was completed, nor that Christianity is the only way to reach God. Thus many Quakers are eager to learn from the members and writings of other Churches and other faiths; dual membership (for example, Quaker and Anglican, Quaker and Buddhist) is not unknown. Quakers are also willing to learn from the sciences and other secular disciplines.

The balance between individual and corporate responsibility has shifted over the centuries: at present the gathered Meeting seems to be becoming more significant again. Add to these factors the normal influences of personality and environment,

including cultural variations in different Yearly Meetings round the world, and it is apparent that moral decisions will not necessarily be uniform. But they will be consistent in the effort to apply the principles of Friends. Friends, therefore, aim to help each other, believing that the process of decision making, when followed faithfully, will lead to the right decision (even if other individuals or groups would have decided differently in apparently similar circumstances). Trusting 'that of God' in everyone is not easy, and they know they fail, but when the process works it is powerful and convincing.

The Roman Catholic Church

Faith community

The pattern of the life of the Church is that of the early church community as described in Acts 2:42 (faithfulness to the Apostles' teaching, to the sacraments, to the common life and to the prayers). The handing on of this life is called the 'tradition' of the Church.

The community is so structured that certain members of the community are ordained to share in a special way in the priesthood of the Church and the priesthood of Christ. Their function is to represent, to teach, and to govern the Christian community. Their priesthood is related to the common priesthood of all the baptised, but is distinct in that it is specifically directed to the 'ordering' of the Church. The Bishops, therefore, are persons in authority, as successors of the Apostles and have 'magisterium' (Latin *magister* meaning 'person in authority').

The teaching function of the Church is exercised in two ways.

1 The Solemn Magisterium

This is exercised through the dogmatic definitions of the Councils of the Church, or the Pope speaking very formally (*ex cathedra*) as chief Bishop in conjunction with all the Bishops of the Church.

2 The ordinary Magisterium

This is the 'day to day' teaching of the Church, and is recognised in the universal practice of the Church, the unanimous consent of the Fathers of the Church (the great teachers, men and women, of history) and of theologians round the world, and in the experience and understanding of the people of God throughout the world. Scripture and tradition form the basis of the Church's teaching.

Scripture

The Scriptures are understood as the word of God in human words. The New Testament can be called the book of the Church. The early community of the Church collected together the records and letters which would be properly recognised as the New Testament. The books would be recognised as the 'canon' of scripture, the norms by which the Church would measure and be measured.

The Church can never go back on God's word. It must always go forward to deepen our understanding of that word revealed in the person of Christ. Christians must try to understand what scripture says, as the word of God in human words. They must seek to understand what kind of human writings they are, in order to discern what God is saying through them today.

Tradition

Right from the beginning the Church developed its understanding of the faith by various means: through debates which led to statements and to creeds and formulas; and through its way of worship and sacramental life. The Catholic Church believes that the Spirit of God is revealing truth through the living out of the Gospel in history. In this sense tradition also reveals the word of God.

Processes

Scripture and tradition are to be seen not as two completely separate elements in the life of the Church, but as complementary and interrelated. They are both parts of the mission to teach given to the Church by Christ. Thus, in brief, the community comes to understanding of new and contemporary problems by an appreciation of all sources of God's self-revelation:

1 the insights of the Scriptures;

2 the tradition of the Church, the way that the Fathers of the Church have reflected on the Scriptures in their own context and history;

3 the wisdom of the scholastic philosophers, who built up a coherent picture relating the Scriptures to human life and thought;

4 the ongoing theological reflection in different parts of the Church in different historical contexts;

5 the contemporary experience of the people of God struggling to live out their faith in justice.

The understanding of, and reflection on, these sources occurs nationally through the local hierarchies in each country, and then internationally through the relationship of the Bishops throughout the world with the Pope in Rome.

Diversity of views

The statements of faith, the dogmas and creeds of the Church are formulas that need to be continually interpreted in the light of human experience to be made relevant to the human situation throughout history. This process of interpretation is the work of the theologian and, as would be expected in contemporary life, it is possible to find a range of interpretations, a range of different 'theologies' in the one community. While sharing the same faith and professing the same creed, it is part of the ongoing richness of the Christian life that there are different ways of understanding and living out the gospel.

One of the functions of a teaching Church is to enable these different theologies to debate and interact with each other and thus come to a richer and deeper appreciation of the word of God in today's world.

But the teaching Church also has to take account of the need for pastoral care. While the Church seeks to proclaim the truth of the Gospel, and give guidance in the Christian way of life with general moral norms, it is also fully aware of the weakness of human nature and at times the apparent impossibility for many of living up to the ideals which are presented as the Christian way of life.

That does not mean the Church will change its teaching, or regard the norm as wrong. Rather the way that it exercises pastoral care of its members reflects a true understanding of the full message of Christ. This is at the heart of the Church's teaching and sacramental way of life. The Church, like St Paul, aims to help Christians discover God's power in their weakness. So if people are not able to measure up to the guidelines offered by the Church, the pastoral care of the Church and a sharing in the Sacraments, especially of Forgiveness, enable them to live with their weakness and to renew their desire to live according to the ideals of the Gospel.

The Salvation Army

Scriptures

For The Salvation Army the authority of the Scriptures is basic to its understanding of moral and social issues. The place of scripture in the teaching of The Salvation Army is contained in one of its fundamental articles of faith:

> We believe that the scriptures of the Old and New Testaments were given by inspiration of God, and that they only constitute the divine rule of Christian faith and practice.

Where clear scriptural teaching is perceived on any subject, any statement by The Salvation Army would be in accordance with such teaching. Where there is no specific teaching in scripture on a given subject, an attempt would be made to interpret the general tenor of scriptural teaching concerning the principles involved.

Tradition

Traditionally, the teaching and beliefs of The Salvation Army have been in line with those of the mainstream Christian Churches. The interpretation of scriptures is in accord with conservative evangelical scholarship, without being fundamentalist. Combined with this is a pragmatic and compassionate response to human need, especially to the victims of social injustice and deprivation. These traditions are still strong, and undoubtedly influence attitudes to moral and social questions.

Congregation involvement

The membership of the Moral and Social Issues Council mentioned under Processes below, represents a cross-section of Salvation Army officers and lay salvationists in the United Kingdom, and is considered qualified to act on behalf of The Salvation Army in this country. Information on topics under discussion is published in Salvation Army periodicals, and input invited. Material received in response to such an invitation would be made known to council members, and taken into account in the discussion.

Local congregations (known as 'corps') might have their own study groups, but they are not actively involved in the formulating process, except as stated above. In exercising discipline or giving pastoral guidance, local leaders would be expected to respond compassionately and sensitively to situations of need or distress, while maintaining the standards set out in official guidelines.

Processes

Statements setting out Salvation Army views on particular social and moral issues are prepared by the Moral and Social Issues Council at the International Headquarters of The Salvation Army in London. In order to make sure that they are in line with general Salvation Army policy, the statements are sent in draft form to the world leader of The Salvation Army and are issued in his or her name. Usually, before approval is given they will be referred for review by an advisory council of senior Salvation Army leaders.

Once the General's approval is given to a statement, it is published in Salvation Army periodicals, and issued as a Press Release, as the official stance on that subject.

The Moral and Social Issues Council is made up of salvationists from all parts of the United Kingdom. Of its twenty-two members, eleven are full time Salvation Army officers. The others are lay salvationists with specialist qualifications, some of them eminent in their particular fields.

Discussions on particular issues usually range over several meetings, and often entail extra research work by sub-groups of the council. The aim is to achieve a consensus of opinion, and so far this has always been achieved, although varying viewpoints are expressed.

Diversity of views

Each salvationist is not expected necessarily to subscribe to everything that a statement on any issue contains. There are, and will continue to be, divergent views held personally on many issues, but the official viewpoint will always be that expressed in the published statement, until it is revised or withdrawn.

There are some ethical issues that come into a more mandatory class, and form part of Salvation Army Orders and Regulations for all full members. For instance, on the issue of the non-medical use of alcohol and other drugs, every member of the world-wide Salvation Army is bound by a ruling that requires total abstinence. Such regulations are reviewed and updated from time to time by various policy-making bodies, but that lies outside the work of the Moral and Social Issues Council.

The United Reformed Church

Scripture

The United Reformed Church (URC) was formed in 1972 by a union of the Congregational Church in England and Wales with the Presbyterian Church of England, enlarged in 1982 by a further union with the Reformed Association of the Churches of Christ and in 2000 by union with the Scottish Congregational Church. Part of the Basis of the Union is 'The Statement concerning the Nature, Faith and Order of the United Reformed Church'. This statement is read aloud and affirmed when a person is ordained for the first time to the Christian ministry within the URC, and is used also at services for the induction of a minister to a new pastorate. Part of it reads:

> The United Reformed Church acknowledges the Word of God in the Old and New Testaments, discerned under the guidance of the Holy Spirit, as the supreme authority for the faith and conduct of all God's people.

Biblical study and reflection are essential elements of Christian decision-making.

Tradition

The URC has had less than thirty years in which to formulate its own tradition, but the particular heritage of each of its participating denominations remains a vital part of that. It stands in the tradition of the Nonconformist Churches in this country, emphasising freedom and openness of thought.

Congregation or faith community

Each local church will frequently make decisions for itself on social and moral issues, particularly in relation to the situation of the community in which it is set. The regular Church Meeting provides a forum for Church Members, that is young people and adults who have publicly confessed their faith and been received into the privileges and responsibilities of membership of the Church. The purpose of these meetings is to enable members to 'have the opportunity through discussion, responsible decision and care for one another, to strengthen each other's faith and to foster the life, work and mission of the Church' (*Basis of Union*). It is at the Church Meeting that the members would decide, for example, about remarrying divorced people, about taking part in local campaigns on social problems and about the local response to decisions taken by the General Assembly of the URC. If there is a particular issue which a local church feels should be drawn to the attention of the URC for action, nationally, a resolution can be taken from a Church Meeting via a District Council and a Synod to the General Assembly (see below).

Processes

The United Reformed Church meets once a year in General Assembly which makes decisions on behalf of the whole Church. There are about 650 members of the Assembly (almost equal numbers lay and ordained) chosen by the District Councils (local groupings of about 25–30 churches) and the thirteen Synods of which all the local congregations are members. The Assembly appoints staff and committees, one of which, Church and Society, advises the Assembly on social and moral questions on which Christian opinion or action is required. The Church and Society Committee prepares reports on various social and moral questions for discussion in the churches and brings matters for decision to the General Assembly and its advisory body, the Mission Council.

The Synods also discuss moral and social questions and sometimes bring matters for consideration by General Assembly, which usually expects to be guided by the Church and Society Committee before reaching a decision. The Committee often consults with local churches through the Synods before forming proposals for decision. For example, guidelines on the remarriage of divorced persons were agreed by the General Assembly after a survey had been carried out among local churches; resolutions about nuclear weapons came to the General Assembly direct from Synods in consultation with Church and Society; and a report on homosexuality was first discussed in a number of churches around the country before being considered by the whole Church.

Diversity of views

The General Assembly is, for the United Reformed Church, 'the central organ of its life and the final authority, under the Word of God and the promised guidance of the Holy Spirit, in all matters of doctrine and order and in all other concerns of its common life' (*Basis of Union*). But it also provides a further opportunity for discussion on moral and social questions. Decisions are reached by majority vote but resolutions on such issues generally include such words as 'recommend', 'encourage', 'urge', and consequently cannot be seen as binding on all URC members. Assembly has always reflected the inevitable differences of opinion within the Church. One example is that, while most URC congregations and ministers are in favour of offering divorced persons the opportunity of remarriage in a church service, there are some congregations and ministers who disagree and their right to do so is respected.

Section 1 • Relationships and Family

The Baptist Union of Great Britain

Baptists believe that God is Trinity, both three and one. The persons of the Trinity, the Father, the Son and the Holy Spirit, love one another. Humans, made in the image of God, reflect God's character and image when they form loving relationships with one another. All relationships are worthwhile and significant and it is a part of the role of the churches to work to make all human relationships more adequate reflections of their divine counterpart. This applies to relationships in marriage, in families, in the churches and in society.

Marriage

Marriage is the means by which the churches recognise the mutual love and commitment of a man and a woman to one another. It is a sign of the love of Christ and the Church for one another and should therefore be something joyful, precious and enduring. Marriages are a sign, albeit an imperfect one, of the presence of a loving God in the world. The churches therefore have a role in preparing people for marriage and in helping marriages to endure.

Since they are patterned on the love between Christ and the Church, marriages are a matter of public interest and are of concern to God. This is the reason we regard only those who have taken public vows in the context of worship as being truly married in the eyes of God. All this makes marriage a serious responsibility, one requiring mutual self-giving and demanding faithfulness. Where marriage is understood in these ways it has a positive effect on those involved and on their children; it also has a beneficial effect on society as a whole.

It is because we have such a high view of marriage that adultery and divorce are regarded so seriously by our churches. Nevertheless, most Baptists recognise that when a marriage has broken down irretrievably, it may do more harm than good both to those directly involved and to those around them. In such circumstances, after all attempts at counselling, mediation and conciliation have failed, Baptists would generally countenance the possibility of divorce.

The breakdown of a marriage gives cause for regret and sadness and calls for support and care for those involved so that healing and forgiveness may follow the trauma of divorce. Where this occurs and due acknowledgement of past sins and failures is made, many Baptists regard subsequent marriages as true marriages.

Family

For many people, their key relationships are those they have with members of their own families. These families may be of many different kinds and sizes: extended families, households, small communities sharing accommodation. The Bible should not be understood to endorse only the nuclear family. In fact, the Old Testament demonstrates that God has a special concern for lone parents and children without fathers. Families of every kind offer the possibility of life in community, of life in relationship with others; it is this that is important, not any one particular model of the family.

Where families work well, the benefits are felt well beyond those actually involved; where they fail, the circumstances affect a similar network of people. Baptists therefore believe that support for families of all kinds should be a priority for public policy and for the churches.

The local church

The Baptist understanding of the Church sees the local church as a community where everyone is committed to building and maintaining right and loving relationships. One purpose of this is to reflect the nature of God and another is to offer a model, albeit a flawed and provisional one, for the rest of society.

The Church of England

Marriage and the family

The Church of England has always valued marriage and family life. It believes that marriage, between a man and a woman, should always be undertaken as a lifelong commitment, and that it provides the proper context for sexual relationships and the bringing up of children.

Marriage is God's gift available to all people. The Church has a responsibility to minister to everyone in this country and to solemnise the marriage of all parishioners who request this ministry. There is ongoing debate in relation to the implications of this for our multi-faith society.

The Church of England marriage ceremony is usually conducted by a member of the clergy in church in the presence of the couple's friends and relatives.

Facing the pressures

There is a concern to sustain and strengthen support for the institution of marriage and family life.

The Church realises that some marriages, sadly, will reach a point of irretrievable breakdown. Whilst clergy have the right under the law of the land to marry divorcees in church, usually second marriages do not take place in church. Although the General Synod recognises some circumstances in which a divorced person may be married in church during the lifetime of a former partner, the procedures for determining when such marriages should be allowed have not yet been agreed.

The General Synod recognises the variety of 'family' relationships that exist in society nowadays and has expressed regret that there is an increase in the numbers of those who live together, either before or instead of marrying.

There is a concern at the prevailing rate of family breakdown and in particular the effect of this on many of the country's children.

The Church of Scotland

Where a man and woman love one another and wish to live together, marriage provides the best and securest foundation for a long and happy relationship. Marriage should be a life-long commitment, and in this context of trusting security men and women engage in sexual relations, knowing that any child conceived will be welcome within a family setting. The Church of Scotland accepts that within

marriage sexual intercourse is not solely or even primarily for the purpose of procreation but serves to enrich relationships.

Living together before marriage does not guarantee a successful marriage. It is left to a minister's own conscience and discretion whether or not to marry a couple who have already been living together and are free to marry.

The Church recognises that people can make mistakes about one another and that for different reasons relationships can break down and turn nasty. In such cases where there is a breakdown which is irreparable, divorce is permissible.

However 'amicable' the divorce proceedings may be, the implications of the split-up can be painful, and the sense of betrayal, fear, and loss experienced at the ending of a relationship should not be underestimated. The stress is not confined to the couple. Children and the extended family, like grandparents, may be affected.

The ease with which a divorce can sometimes be obtained means that for some it is taken as the way out, when there may be a need to address some deep-seated personal questions. For such people, unless the fundamental problems are sorted out, the prospect is that they will enter another relationship which may prove no more satisfactory.

After consultation with the minister a divorced person may be married in the Church if Scotland. Christ meets people where they are so the Church has to be alongside the divorcee, the lone parent, the hurt child, demonstrating unconditional love and acceptance. Christians are called to love, not to be judgmental.

The Methodist Church

Marriage and the family

According to Methodist teaching, marriage is 'the life-long union in body, mind and spirit of one man and one woman'. The union of man and woman for companionship and mutual support, in equal partnership, and the procreation and bringing up of children, is held by the Church to be God's gift and God's will for most men and women.

Sexuality is a gift of God, which is to be received with joy. It is central to the renewal, deepening and enjoyment of the marriage relationship. To establish and maintain a home is one of the greatest creative acts in which men and women can engage. All couples who seek to be married in a Methodist Church will be welcomed into a period of preparation in which the Church's convictions about marriage are clarified and opportunities are given for growth in self-understanding and development of their relationship.

However, the family is not an end in itself; while parents are to be 'honoured', most of us leave one home to found another, either with others or as a single person. Methodists believe that human fulfilment is possible without marriage and indeed without engaging in sexual intercourse. Singleness offers opportunities for friendship and service which are not open to married people. The Methodist Church teaches that sexual intercourse belongs within marriage.

Divorce

Christian teaching is that marriage is the life-long union of the partners, and is therefore in principle indissoluble. However, with other Christians, the Methodist Church recognises that for a variety of reasons marriages can die. They can become destructive rather than creative experiences for all concerned. After making every effort to save the relationship, and taking care of the interests and future of children of the marriage, separation or divorce may be unavoidable.

Where a local church is in touch with one or both of the parties to a failed marriage, the offer of new life and the healing of memories is to be made. The possibility of new relationships and, where appropriate, a new marriage, is to be welcomed.

A minister who conscientiously objects to the marriage of divorced persons is not personally required to conduct the wedding of a couple involving one or more divorced persons.

Basis: Conference Statement on *A Christian Understanding of Family Life, the Single Person and Marriage* (1992) and *Christian Preparation for Marriage* (1998).

The Religious Society of Friends (Quakers)

Marriage

'Marriage has always been regarded by Friends as a religious commitment rather than merely a civil contract.' (*Advices and Queries* 1995) In 1669, George Fox described the Quaker view of marriage:

> The right joining in marriage is the work of the Lord only, and not the priest's or magistrate's; for it is God's ordinance and not man's . . we marry none; it is the Lord's work, and we are but witnesses.

Nonetheless, early Quakers recognised the importance of recording marriages and accepted their responsibility for reporting such marriages to the authorities. As early as 1661, Quaker weddings were legally recognised. Indeed, until the Marriage Act of 1836 only Quakers and Jews were permitted to marry outside the Established Church (subject to various regulations). During the eighteenth and early nineteenth century, marriage to a non-Quaker, known as 'marrying out', or a non-Quaker wedding, was seen as cause for 'disownment' (exclusion from membership). Happily modern Quakers are not so inward looking.

Nowadays, when a couple wish to marry in the Quaker way, usually one or both of them will have a close association with a local Meeting. This is for two reasons: firstly there may be legal requirements to be met, especially in Scotland; secondly, and more importantly, it is so that the Meeting can offer its prayerful care and support to the couple, in the time of preparation for their marriage, during the wedding and during their married life. It is difficult to give that kind of care to people who are strangers, or who do not have the same understanding of 'marriage in the care of a Friend's Meeting.'

The couple will probably talk to their local overseers (who are appointed to offer pastoral care); they may ask for a 'meeting for clearness' to help them prepare for their marriage. When ready, they apply to the registering officer of the Monthly Meeting. Once the Monthly Meeting has approved the application for marriage, the registering officer, who is recognised by law, makes arrangements for the public notices and other legal requirements.

A Quaker wedding is a meeting for worship for the couple, together with their friends. They gather in worship to make a commitment to each other in the presence of God. The couple take each other freely and equally as life-long partners, committing themselves to joining their lives together in loving companionship and asking God's blessing on their union.

The wedding will be very informal compared with weddings from other traditions. The bride and groom may greet the guests, then quietly slip into the meeting room along with their friends or they may come in when everybody else is seated. Near the couple will be a table with the Quaker wedding certificate and a pen. The couple will be dressed simply. Some Quaker brides wear white, but many do not, preferring to wear something that can be worn again on other occasions.

At the start someone will explain briefly what is going to happen; then the meeting will settle into silence. After ten to fifteen minutes, the bride and groom stand and take it in turns to make their promises, while holding each other by the hand:

> Friends, I take this my Friend, [full name], to be my husband/wife, promising through divine assistance, to be unto him/her a loving and faithful wife/husband, so long as we both on earth shall live.

There are some variations possible in the wording: for example, 'with God's help' and 'until it shall please the Lord by death to separate us'. Then the couple sign the wedding certificate, which records their promises, followed by two witnesses (often the parents), and then the registering officer reads out the whole certificate. Everyone present is responsible for witnessing and upholding the marriage so everyone will sign the certificate, even the youngest child, but as this can take a long time to complete it is usually done after the meeting for worship.

During the next half hour or so anyone who feels moved to may speak, offer a prayer or a reading, just as in a normal meeting for worship. The meeting ends when the elders shake hands.

After the meeting the couple sign the Civil Register. Sometimes Quaker women will keep their own surnames as a witness to the equality of the sexes. Traditionally, Quakers did not wear wedding rings but nowadays many Quakers do exchange rings. The reception will usually be held at the meeting house so there will be no alcohol.

Divorce and remarriage

If Quakers were experiencing difficulties in a relationship they might turn to the following Advice:

> A long term relationship brings both fulfilment and tension. If your relationship with a partner is under strain, seek help in exploring your own feelings, which may be powerful and destructive, and in discerning God's guidance for you. If you undergo the distress of separation and divorce, try to maintain some compassionate communication so that arrangements can be made with the minimum of bitterness. In arrangements made for children, seek to hear and consider their wishes and remember their enduring need for love and security.

> ---
> *Advices and Queries*, 1995

When a divorce occurs the members of the meeting will try to offer love and support to each partner. They will try to help the couple separate with respect and care for each other and any children.

If divorced people want to marry in the care of the Meeting, the registering officer will need to know that they are legally free to do so. The Monthly Meeting will need to be sure that they are clear of past commitments, and really ready to enter a new marriage, with its solemn life-long promise, and that the situation and feelings of any children have been fully considered. The meeting will take advice from the overseers.

Sex outside marriage

Sex outside marriage does take place – Quakers are not isolated from changes in social attitudes. A discussion document published in 1963 called *Towards a Quaker View of Sex* posed many questions, which are still being considered. However, though there is much wider recognition now than, say, 50 years ago that a couple can be faithful to each other in a loving, non-exploitative relationship outside marriage, Quakers have not yet decided to change the marriage regulations, which still see marriage as something different – God's work, to use George Fox's words

Children and young people

Children have always played an important part in Quakerism ever since the children and young women of Reading and Stourbridge Meetings 'kept' their Meetings by faithfully attending worship while the adults were imprisoned during the 1660s. Today Friends recognise that all members of their meetings, of whatever age, have a role to play in upholding the life and worship of the Society. The *Advices and Queries* 1995 say:

> Rejoice in the presence of children and young people in your meeting and recognise the gifts they bring Remember that the meeting as a whole shares a responsibility for every child in its care. Seek for them as for yourself a full development of God's gifts and the abundant life Jesus tells us can be ours. How do you share your deepest beliefs with them, while leaving them free to develop as the spirit of God may lead them? Do you invite them to share their insights with you? Are you ready both to learn from them and to accept your responsibilities towards them?

Even the smallest children are welcome in meetings and their noise and chatter may spark some spoken ministry by an adult. Small children quickly learn what is needed of them in coming into the silent meeting. They will spend part of the hour in their own Children's Meeting and about fifteen minutes in Meeting for Worship (either at the beginning or the end). Parents may try to help their children to become accustomed to silence at home – for instance in a silent 'grace' before meals, or a moment of quiet before being tucked up for the night. Parents will also try to give some guidance on what to do in the silent meeting for worship – perhaps saying 'thank you' to God for something good that has happened or looking round at each person present and silently asking God to take care of them or, afterwards, talking together about the Meeting.

Quaker parents will not seek to impose their views or beliefs but will encourage their children to discuss, enquire, listen and reflect. They may well develop interests in issues such as non-violence or homelessness and at times their concerns can set them apart from other children in their neighbourhood. When there are only one or two Quaker pupils in a school they can feel quite isolated and may have a difficult time trying to defend daily a peace testimony which they may not yet have fully worked through for themselves. The Children's Meeting and Link Groups for teenagers are two of the ways in which Quaker young people can be supported.

Different life-styles

Quakers recognise that many of their own children are not in married relationships: for example, sons or daughters caring for aged parents, friends who share a home for many years, widows or widowers, divorced or separated people, single parents, and those in homosexual relationships.

> All of us, partnered or single, need to feel that we belong, that we are valued and included – we need affirmation and recognition of who and what we are – we need, in our meeting especially, to make sure that this happens.
>
> ———————————
>
> *Quaker Faith and Practice*, 1995

Violence and abuse in relationships

Quakers believe that there is that of God in everyone and they try to express that belief in practice. This means, for example, that Quakers are on the whole pacifists who will not kill another person for any reason. They put their efforts into prevention, in trying to eliminate the causes of violence, and in trying to heal the wounds when violence and conflict have, in fact, occurred. Similarly with violence in personal relationships, they try to support families, so that they are loving and caring, not exploitative.

Although Friends have not issued a corporate statement about child abuse, there is no question in their minds that it is wrong. If they became aware of a case in their midst they would take steps to protect and support the child. In children's and young people's groups they try to have the kind of open and trusting atmosphere where children and young adults could speak about problems if they needed to. In Meetings it is likely that there will be adults who are trained as teachers, social workers, Samaritans or Relate counsellors who would be able to help young people if they asked for help. Friends have given careful thought to the need for protection of children in any activities organised and have issued a booklet entitled *Health, Safety and the Law*.

What about attitudes to the abuser? It is hard to think that an abuser also has that of God in him or her, yet if Quakers really believe that people can be healed, that they can learn to be good and loving people eventually, then they have to try and make the effort. They hope that if the abuser were a Quaker and sent to prison, somebody in the Meeting would keep in touch, writing letters and visiting, trying to encourage a realisation of the wrong that had been done so that they could grow towards repentance and forgiveness.

The Roman Catholic Church

In *Familiaris Consortio* John Paul II emphasises the importance of marriage as an 'intimate partnership of life and love' (*Gaudium et Spes*) entered into with free consent – open to the possibility of welcoming children to create a community: 'the domestic church'.

Speaking of the ideal, the Pope points to the role of the family in 'humanising and personalising society' by being a forum for the celebration of personal dignity, individuality, the cultivation of authentic values (truth, freedom, justice, love) and the development of a sense of 'humanity', in each member, encouraging them to contribute to a civilisation of love which is characterised by a preferential option for the poor within society locally, nationally and internationally.

However, we know that not all interpersonal relationships run smoothly and families can become fragmented. Those whose marital tensions end tragically in the trauma of divorce are to be offered wide-ranging support and encouraged to take an active part in church life. But neither husband nor wife are able to have a second marriage blessed if the partner of the first marriage still survives – unless there are reasons to believe that the first relationship lacked some essential quality which meant that the couple did not actually fulfil all that was required for it to be a valid marriage when the facts surrounding it are examined by a tribunal. This is a complex and painful matter for all members of the family and requires great pastoral sensitivity on the part of the Church.

The rights of the family to housing, education, health care, social benefit schemes, religious freedom, security and opportunities to travel freely are upheld in the *Catechism of the Catholic Church* (CCC §2211).

In the introduction to the Catholic Bishops' of England and Wales document entitled 'The Common Good,' both the central theme and overall context for the church's understanding of 'family' in its broadest terms – domestic, community-based and world-wide – is outlined:

> The foundation of this teaching is the dignity of the human person. In virtue simply of our shared humanity, we must surely respect and honour one another. Each individual has a value that can never be lost and must never be ignored. Moreover, each one of us is made in the image and likeness of God. Society must therefore first of all respect and protect human life itself – at all its stages from conception to its natural end.

The Salvation Army

The family – God's idea

The family is seen in scripture, for the protection, nurturing and development of each individual. The Salvation Army seeks to promote family life and to play whatever role it can in preventing its breakdown or demise. Jesus Christ became a member of a human family; therefore God affirmed family life and revealed again his will for the role of the family in the right ordering of human affairs.

Concepts of the family

The word 'family' can be understood to mean

1 the nuclear family (mother, father and any children), or

2 the wider kinship groups extending within and across several generations – the extended family.

This second concept plays a prominent part in many non-Western cultures.

Therefore the Army views the opportunity for establishing a family based on marriage, as a basic human right.

Marriage and family

All cultures and societies have recognised the innate need of the human race to protect its young. Similarly, all cultures and societies have some form of bonding between potential parents, recognised by the community and known generally as marriage.

In Western society, thinking about family life has meant monogamous marriage, defined as the union for life of one man and one woman to the exclusion of all others, marked by an authorised ceremony, whether religious or civil or both.

The Salvation Army believes that family life, based on marriage, is the bedrock of a stable society and wishes to do all it can to promote families and marriages. The Army seeks to influence legislators to take steps to protect family life, and to discourage negative models and images of marriage and family life in the media.

Cohabiting without marriage

The Salvation Army is aware that many today choose to live together, as though husband and wife, without marriage. However, it believes that such a relationship still falls short of God's ideal will.

This, as revealed in scripture, is for sexual union to be expressed in the context of marriage. Resulting children can then be nurtured in the knowledge that their biological parents, or adoptive parents if this is the case, are mutually committed in this way. The emotional, psychological and physical security flowing from this is likely to afford the most helpful environment for their upbringing.

Cohabiting without marriage is not in the best interests of society, individual partners or their offspring. Nevertheless, the Army readily assists people, materially and spiritually, who adopt this life-style, while not condoning the life-style itself.

One parent families

The Salvation Army is keenly aware and sensitively conscious of those many family units in which a parent is forced by circumstances to raise a family, for example following bereavement, divorce or legal separation. To these family units The Army offers support and care.

It regrets that a minority of people deliberately set out to create one-parent families, which cannot be in the best interests of the child. To these families The

Army gives help when needed, whilst avoiding anything likely to condone or encourage their actions.

Family breakdown

The Salvation Army works widely with couples experiencing marital difficulties and with families under stress. It is realistic about the frailty of human nature and recognises that some marriages fail.

The Army seeks to promote high standards in marriage and in family life, through its teaching and preaching ministries and by its programmes for social and community service.

It recognises that the sense of belonging which begins with family can lead to a sense of belonging to the community and ultimately to an awareness of belonging to God.

Taken from Positional Statement 13, January 1994.

The United Reformed Church

Remarriage

When a Christian marriage takes place, it is not a relationship entered into lightly but with a deep sense of love, life-long commitment, holiness and joy. If such a marriage breaks down, it is after much agonising and with a feeling that the relationship has ceased to be creative.

In such circumstances the church will be concerned to seek a reconciliation because Christian marriage is ideally a life-long relationship which can overcome difficulties. When reconciliation proves impossible and the marriage ends in divorce, the church has a pastoral role in relation to the former marriage partners. They often feel a deep sense of failure and experience loneliness. Church members sometimes add to these burdens by lack of understanding and concern.

Christ taught the ideal in all aspects of human life but he had a deep compassion for those who failed to attain the ideal and who recognised and regretted their failure. The church also needs to show compassion for those who fail to maintain the ideal in a marriage relationship but who still hold a Christian view of marriage.

Since the church upholds the ideal of Christian marriage as a life-long relationship, it follows that any request for remarriage after divorce must be given careful and prayerful consideration. Some ministers and churches refuse on grounds of their interpretation of scriptural teaching to conduct any remarriage service after divorce, and their consciences ought to be respected.

In general, within the United Reformed Church such marriages are allowed in certain circumstances.

In the first place, the previous marriage must be dissolved. In all cases the legal contract must have been terminated by the State. Secondly, the minister will wish usually to discuss the circumstances surrounding the breakdown of the previous marriage and the satisfactory resolution of any resulting problems, particularly the care of children. Thirdly, some divorcees and some ministers and churches may wish to have a service in which penitence can be expressed for the failure of the previous marriage, recognition be given that the relationship is now ended and the desire to seek a new beginning made explicit.

When the minister and the church are satisfied that the circumstances are right, a divorcee may be married in church. It will be made clear that the service is a Christian marriage service and therefore the ideal of a life-long union is involved. The service will differ little, if at all, from the normal marriage service. This underlines the necessity, as for a first marriage, of careful preparation before the service and a continuing pastoral relationship, when possible, after the service.

When the circumstances seem right for a marriage involving a divorcee, but where the local minister or church cannot consider it on grounds of conscience, arrangements should be made within the Synod to enable the couple to be interviewed and to be married within the United Reformed Church if that is possible.

There is no contribution from The Russian Orthodox Church in this section

Section 2 • The Beginning of Life

The Baptist Union of Great Britain

Baptists believe in the sanctity of human life and the need to preserve human relationships with God, each other and the world. Baptists are deeply concerned to protect the life of the innocent foetus in both the forms of contraception and abortion. There is a recognition that taking life may be the lesser of evils in situations of rape, incest and particular threat to the well-being of the mother, the foetus and the wider family.

Contraception is a gift from medical science under God's sovereignty. Contraceptive decisions will always consider the impact on human life from the earliest stages. Many regard the abortifacient function of Intra Uterine Devices and various contraceptive pills as taking human life and therefore to be avoided. Control over fertility is a matter for a couple's conscientious decision in light of scripture and tradition, before God. Choosing not to have or to space families is a morally defensible choice, considering the needs of the world, population size, a couple's responsibilities to each other and to potential and living children.

If life is seen as beginning at fertilisation, certain contraceptive methods will be morally repugnant, though might be a necessary evil. If life begins at implantation, then the scope of contraceptive methods is much wider.

Baptists have a broad range of opinion about the beginning of human life and the value attached to that life as it develops. Most wish the law permitting abortion to be more tightly constructed and the time limit of abortion (currently 24 weeks) to be lowered as far as possible. Few absolutely reject abortion in all circumstances, recognising that in a fallen world it may be a lesser of two evils. Far better to prevent the conditions which lead to the necessity of abortion.

Infertility is both a disease and a cause of dis-ease. Technologies of in-vitro fertilisation involving union of sperm and egg cause concern over the creation of 'spare' embryos, their storage and the use of human material for experimental work. While recognising the difference between an embryo with the potential to develop fully into a human being and a child, the embryo must be protected from harm. The extent of such protection is debated, but the use and disposal of human life always requires sound justification and appropriate respect.

Baptist communities seek to support all who face hard choices over beginning of life issues, regardless of what they decide.

The Church of England

For Christians, two premises underpin the issues of contraception, abortion, human fertilisation and embryology. These have been reaffirmed by the General Synod:

- All human life, including life developing in the womb, is created by God in his own image and is therefore to be nurtured, supported and protected.

- Marriage is the ideal context for the procreation and rearing of children.

Conception

To conceive a child by means of sexual intercourse within the context of a Christian marriage is to fulfil one of the God-given purposes of marriage.

Contraception

Sexual love is seen as good in itself, and provides an essential way for a husband and wife to express and strengthen their love for each other. The Church of England accepts contraception as a means of enabling a couple to enjoy sex and to take responsibility for the size of their family.

Abortion

The Church of England combines strong opposition to abortion with a recognition that there can be strictly limited conditions under which it may be morally legitimate. For example, when the continuance of a pregnancy threatens the life of the mother, abortion may be justified. The General Synod has urged that any necessary abortion is carried out as early in the pregnancy as possible. On the rare occasion when abortion is carried out beyond 24 weeks, 'serious foetal handicap' should be interpreted strictly as applying to those conditions where survival is possible only for a very short period. General Synod resolutions, however, inevitably leave many questions unanswered. In difficult cases, such as conception as a result of rape, or the foetus being at risk of serious handicap, Anglicans agree on the need to have regard to 'compassion for the mother and a proper responsibility for the life of the unborn child'. It is possible that they may come to different conclusions about the proper course of action in particular cases.

The General Synod urges that abortion law should be applied more strictly and the number of abortions should be drastically reduced.

The Church is committed to create a caring climate in which real alternatives to abortion are available, to develop educational programmes which promote understanding of human sexuality and relationships, and to offer spiritual, moral and practical support to those who have to meet the challenge of parenthood in difficult circumstances.

Assisted conception

The development of medical techniques for assisting conception has raised complex ethical issues. There is a need to consider the moral connection between marriage, sexual intercourse, conception, birth and the nurturing of children. The simplistic notion that what was 'natural' was 'right' and what was 'unnatural' (or even, perhaps, unusual) was 'wrong' has been challenged by the development of techniques for assisted conception, such as artificial insemination, in-vitro fertilisation, cryopreservation, embryo, sperm and ovum donations.

In relation to these, four sets of problems need to be considered carefully:

• the morality of the action itself
• its legal consequences
• the genetic element
• the personal consequences to the child.

For detailed consideration of the moral, philosophical and theological implications of these techniques, see *Personal Origins* (1996, Church House Publishing).

The Church of Scotland

Contraception

The use of contraception within marriage is part of a Christian's response both to the needs of home and family, and to the needs of a world where an ever-growing population puts an increasing pressure on resources. However the liberal issue of contraceptives to young people irrespective of age has led to an increase in sexually transmitted diseases and far from helping people develop more fulfilling relationships may even make any eventual stable relationships more difficult. Sex education must be primarily about self-understanding, self-respect and respect for others, and the ways of developing meaningful relationships. Contraceptive pills used after intercourse may raise the question of abortion.

Abortion

It is widely held within the Church of Scotland that in the great majority of cases abortion has no moral justification and represents the unwarranted destruction of human life. It has been agreed that the law should embody the principle that the continuance of the pregnancy would involve serious risk to the life, or grave injury to the health, whether physical or mental, of the pregnant woman. This view would hold that the principle of the relief of suffering would justify the use of abortion. However some would also say that in certain circumstances, for example following rape, incest, or where a foetal abnormality had been diagnosed, abortion would be ethically acceptable.

The church recognises that many doctors would see themselves as having a two-fold obligation – to save life and to relieve suffering – and that some of the most difficult ethical issues arise when these conflict so that the right to life of the unborn child has to be forfeited to relieve the suffering of the mother. Other doctors see the sanctity of life as absolute. It cannot be set aside even in the interests of relieving suffering. In every case counselling opportunities should be made more available before and after any abortion is undergone.

If any alternatives to abortion are to carry conviction the Church must face the difficulties that there may be in providing after-care and long-term support both for those who go through with a termination and for those who decide against it and are left to cope with stressful economic or personal social circumstances, caring, for example, with a severely disabled child.

Reproductive engineering

In considering the needs and desires of those who want to have a child there are some basic questions which first have to be asked, for example: 'Do all couples have a fundamental right to have a child if they so wish? Is there a parental instinct that has to be satisfied? If we answer 'Yes' to these questions, would that apply to couples who are not married, to homosexual couples, and to someone who is single? Then there is the matter of costs. Should a Health Service spend money on this and neglect the treatment of fatal diseases?

As a result of drugs being used to increase fertility spare embryos are often created. How long have these to be kept in storage? To whom do they belong? Who decides when they are to be destroyed? Where embryos have been collected from a couple should they be implanted in the woman where the husband or partner has died? Should donors be allowed to sell spare embryos for research purposes?

By law, before anyone is given licensed treatment or consents to the use or storage of embryos, he or she must be given 'such relevant information as is proper'. Such information should cover such things as possible outcomes of treatment, risks of techniques involved, and the legal position. Where medical examination involves the possible discovery of genetic problems it is essential that people are given such help. Counselling should always help people to move on to a better understanding of themselves and what they are doing.

In conclusion the Church of Scotland:

1 affirms the sanctity of the embryo from conception, and urges that its special nature be recognised in law;

2 welcomes the limitation of research on human embryos to fourteen days, and opposes any extension of that limit;

3 recognises that IVF treatment may be right for married couples and for unmarried couples in

faithful, stable, lasting relationships, where gametes used are those of both partners;

4 opposes donor insemination and IVF treatment where either the sperm or the egg are donated;

5 opposes the offer of infertility treatment to those in same sex relationships;

6 opposes surrogacy;

7 opposes gene manipulation and sex selection, except to prevent sex-linked genetic disease.

The Methodist Church

Abortion

Christians believe that human beings are created in God's image. All human life should therefore be reverenced.

The result of the coming together of human sperm and ovum is obviously human. The appearance of the 'primitive streak' (the beginning of the neurological system) after some fourteen days is an important stage. However for many weeks after this event, natural abortion will continue to bring about the termination of over 50% of embryos.

Fertilisation, implantation and subsequent development are parts of a continuous process. It is simply not possible to identify the single moment when a new human person begins. The right of the embryo to full respect clearly increases throughout a pregnancy.

The Methodist Conference Statement of 1976 states that abortion is always an evil, to be avoided if at all possible by offering care to single mothers during pregnancy, and the adoption of their children if, at full term, the mother cannot offer a home. However, the Statement also holds that there will be circumstances where the termination of pregnancy may be the lesser of evils. These include situations where the embryo is grievously handicapped, the pregnancy is the result of rape or the health, mental or physical, of the mother is at risk.

It would be strongly preferable that, through advances in medical science and social welfare, all abortions should become unnecessary. But termination as early as possible in the course of the pregnancy may be the lesser of evils. If abortion were made a criminal offence again, there would be increased risks of ill-health and death as a result of botched 'back-street' abortions. Late abortions should be very rare exceptions. To refuse to countenance abortion in any circumstances is to condemn some women and their babies to gross suffering and a cruel death in the name of an absolutism which nature itself does not observe.

Counselling and pastoral care should be available to the mother and, where the father is known, to the father. The mother should be told clearly of the alternatives to termination.

Contraception

The Methodist Church believes that responsible contraception is a welcome means towards fulfilment in marriage, the spacing of children, and the need to avoid pregnancy altogether, for example for medical reasons.

Basis: *Status of the Unborn Human* 1991; *Statement on Abortion* 1976; *Pastoral Issues on which Guidance is Sought* 1992, Methodist Conference.

The Russian Orthodox Church

Conception

Orthodox Christians profess that all life comes from God and that human life represents his most precious gift. In his creation, man is given the imprint of God's own image and likeness; Adam's fall shattered the image and tarnished the likeness but through our Lord Jesus Christ's incarnation, life, death and resurrection, the image is mended and a likeness restored. This means that our human existence and personhood mirrors the Divine; each person has the potential of growing more and more like God until union with him is attained.

From the moment of conception, such a person exists. The early Fathers of the church were clear that a child *in utero* deserved protection from the moment of conception. St Gregory of Nyssa taught that 'we must think that the point of commencement of existence is one and the same for body and soul'. In other words, the embryo is 'ensouled' from the moment of fertilisation. St Basil the Great added to this by saying ' ... we do not have a precise distinc-

tion between a foetus which has been formed and one which has not yet been formed'.

This gives us an immediate and clear view of recent developments in human experimentation with fertilised human eggs. Destruction and manipulation of such an 'ensouled' fertilised human embryo is contrary to our great ethical tradition.

Contraception

In the Orthodox Church, there are two approaches to contraception, one which fits a well-rounded Orthodox Christian view of the truth and a second, following the path of influence of monasticism, which sees sex as not quite fitting the life of an ascetic Christian except for the purpose of procreating children. Both views derive from firm traditions in the history of the Church.

The first approach, supported by leading modern Orthodox theologians, is summarised by Father Stanley Harakas. Here the emphasis for the meaning of sex in general and conception in particular is placed on the whole experience of marriage as a holy, interpersonal relationship within the total framework of Christian life. Marriage and the sex within it has many purposes, none of which is seen as the crucial and exclusive purpose. Sexual relationships between husband and wife are both procreative and unitive. They have an intrinsic value: they unite husband and wife in flesh and soul in a bond of mutual love and commitment. There is a procreative purpose but when children have been born, and the task is now the nurture of these children in a family environment of mutual love, then the sexual relationship contributes to the tenor and well-being of the family life. Within this perspective, contraception is not condemned but is seen as a means for the fulfilling of the goals and purposes of the marriage as understood by the Church. Normally, however, it would be wrong to use contraception to avoid the birth of any children. This would be seen as selfish and a resistance to God's loving providence.

The second approach, reflecting a more ascetic stance, places sexual relationships for the intended purpose of conceiving children but regards the pleasurable aspects as undesirable. Hence, from this view, contraception is unnecessary and, indeed, is thought to be wrong.

Finally, it should be clearly stated that sexual relations outside marriage are considered to be sinful and the use of contraceptives merely compounds the impropriety of that kind of behaviour.

Abortion

In Orthodox teaching, all life created in the image of God and bearing his likeness must be revered and respected. From the moment of conception there are now two individual lives, mother and child, to be considered. Each one is afforded dignity and respect and it is the duty of society to protect the unborn child. For this reason, the Church condemns abortion except in rare and special cases.

The Fathers of the Church were unanimous in their view that the destruction of a child conceived in the womb is a form of murder and there is no juncture in the life of a developing foetus when this is not so. One early writer, Tertullian, stated: 'Abortion is a precipitation of murder, nor does it matter whether or not one takes a life when formed, or drives it away when forming, for he is also a man who is about to be one'.

Human life is a wonderful gift from God. It is precious and sacred. The value which God places on life is emphasised by his great love for us: 'He gave his only begotten son, that whosoever believes in him, should not perish but have eternal life' (John 3:16). The taking of all life is forbidden (see the story of Cain and Abel in Genesis 4:1–6 and the fifth commandment). The Church upholds the sanctity of life even further in the light of the incarnation of Christ who by becoming man has sanctified all human life both in its spiritual and physical aspects.

At the all-American Council of the Orthodox Church in America in 1973, it was stated that recent attitudes to abortion have created one of the most serious social moral problems facing society. The whole meaning and context of life is being reduced to selfish pursuit of material goals, external success, gratification of senses without regard for the sanctity of God-given life. This undermines the very foundations of society and transgresses divine command.

Only rarely is abortion allowed, when, for example, the mother's life is in danger or her health is seriously threatened. In other circumstances, the life of a child must be preserved and protected as far as is humanly possible. Any decision to have an abortion should be made by the woman in consultation with her medical and spiritual advisors as well as the father of the child. In cases of rape and incest, the Church recognises an 'evil conception'. In these circumstances it is urged that medical advice be sought as soon as possible to prevent implantation (no longer than three days after impregnation). Once implantation occurs, however, the pregnant woman should carry the child to term, and the alternative of adoption should be approached in a spirit of Christian love. Where a woman cannot care for her child, it is the duty of the Church and society to help her or to provide alternative means for the care of the child. Support should be provided for the unmarried mother and for those whose circumstances are desperate. It is not reasonable to insist on the necessity to avoid abortion if society and the Church does not at the same time provide an environment of Christian nurture and safety for both mother and child. What of those women who, because of human frailty and the failure of society, have sought for abortion? They should be received back into the Christian fold in a spirit of love and forgiveness, for we are all subject to sin.

In the preface, we have mentioned the principle of oikonomia as an expression of the love and compassion of God motivated by sympathy and understanding of human weakness. This compels us to reach out to every woman in distress and consider what help should be given. There must be much prayer, heart-searching and self-humbling before the presence of God. Support must be given to women who find themselves in an unbearable and untenable situation. Respect should be afforded to Christian gynaecologists, priests and others who stand with them. Sometimes unacceptable decisions have to be made.

In-vitro fertilisation

The Orthodox Church affirms the duty of the procreation of the human race. God commanded that man 'be fruitful and multiply and fill the earth' (Genesis 1:28). The Church also stresses the sacramental character of Christian marriage: in the Sacrament of Matrimony, marriage enters the realm of God's eternal kingdom. Within its bounds, husband and wife are called to perfect their love for one another and to grow in oneness with Christ. As the Christian man and wife progress in love, they find themselves growing closer, both to each other and to God. The eventual birth of their children is an eloquent and significant expression and seal of their loving union. Offspring represent not only the physical union of husband and wife, but also in their spiritual union and the presence of God, the one true source of love in their marriage. Here they share with God in the creation in new human beings. Artificial insemination preserves the sacramental unity of marriage and the family as long as no foreign party sunders the unique bond between husband and wife. Genetic material from a third party violates the principles of Christian marriage.

In-vitro fertilisation (test tube babies) presents serious problems to the Orthodox conscience. In this procedure, fertilised eggs are kept in a laboratory culture and more eggs are fertilised than can be used. These are later discarded and hence there is a killing of potential life, an abortion. Therefore, in its usual form, this procedure is contrary to Orthodox tradition. The use of a single egg only would be acceptable.

These are moral principles based on Divine Law which guide Orthodox Christians. We do not attempt to impose these laws on others who are not of the household of faith; indeed, we recognise that when men and women persist in behaviour which leads to their estrangement from God, there is often a need for the use of contraception and other measures to safeguard health and to prevent greater catastrophe. Christian gynaecologists at the sharp end of the decision-making process, do not accede to abortion on demand but seek to reach out to women in great distress as they wrestle with overwhelming psychological, social and health-undermining problems. The principle of permitting the lesser of two evils becomes understandable in these circumstances.

The Religious Society of Friends (Quakers)

Contraception

In *Quaker Views No. 4*, one of a series of leaflets for pupils to help them understand the Quaker approach to ethics, reference is made to contraception:

> Quakers have not issued a statement about contraception and family planning. Many Quaker couples do use contraception, preferring to plan the size of their family.

This may be for a variety of reasons – perhaps because they feel they can offer more love and attention to a smaller family, perhaps because they are concerned about the growth in world population or because of their concern for women to be freed to play a full role in society. It is quite common for male Quakers to choose to have a vasectomy rather than leaving the responsibility for contraception to the woman. On the other hand, some Quakers choose not to use contraception, preferring to let nature take its course, or use one of the modern 'natural' methods of avoiding sex at periods of peak fertility. It is a matter for personal choice and conscience.

Abortion

Quakers have not (yet) been led to make a corporate statement on abortion. The *Quaker Views No. 4* leaflet states:

> Quakers have not issued a corporate statement on abortion. This may seem strange from a church that has a strong peace testimony – it would be logical for us to be opposed to abortion. We frequently quote our belief in 'that of God in everyone' so doesn't that mean that there is 'that of God' in the foetus too? A key question here is, 'When does a person become a person?' but Quakers, like many others, have no easy single answer.

There are some Quakers who are opposed to abortion, perhaps for the reasons mentioned above. But there are also other Quakers who are very keen to enable women to play a full role in society. This might lead them to feel, reluctantly and sadly, that in some circumstances abortion may be the only alternative. A question to consider here is whether it is right or wrong to value the life of the unborn child over and above the life of the mother. Personal conscience in the issue is of the greatest importance.

The Roman Catholic Church

Catholic teaching on bioethics

A Roman Catholic perspective on bioethics (moral issues arising from the biological sciences and medical care) draws on the following sources:

- Scripture (both the Old and the New Testament)
- Tradition (all the Church is and believes)
- Reason (philosophical ethics – especially natural law)
- Experience (looking at what happens in real life).

Scripture and tradition are the two principle lenses which we put on our 'microscope' when we examine moral issues. We apply reason and experience in the light of them. Scientific and technological developments can either enhance or threaten the dignity of the human person and so need to be carefully assessed.

Abortion

The tradition and accumulated wisdom of the Church especially includes the documents resulting from the teaching authority or *magisterium* of the Pope and the College of Bishops. The document entitled Declaration on Procured Abortion (*Quaestion de Abortu*, 1974) shows us how the four sources of Catholic teaching are used to address issues surrounding the beginning of life. In Articles 5–8 the basis in Scripture and Tradition for the church's opposition to abortion is reviewed under the heading 'In the Light of Faith'. Articles 8–13 outline what is understood by the nature of the human person and his or her fundamental right to life from the moment of conception with reference to scientific data under the heading 'In the Additional Light of Reason'.

The *Cathechism of the Catholic Church* (CCC) states:

> From the first moment of his (her) existence, a human being must be recognised as having the rights of a person – among which is the inviolable right of every innocent being to life. (CCC §2270)

> Since the first century the Church has affirmed the moral evil of every procured abortion. The teaching has not changed and remains unchangeable. (CCC §2271)

New reproductive technologies

As has been noted, technological developments bring with them important questions about human rights, for example:

- in-vitro fertilisation – the status of the embryo;

- artificial insemination – the meaning of procreation and the concept of parenthood;

- the storage of sperm and eggs – the right to know your parents.

The Church, whilst recognising the painfulness for married couples of not being able to have children, says that a child is a gift not a right. Therefore, care has to be taken that any techniques to assist conception must respect both the integrity of a married relationship (so no use of donor [third party] sperm or eggs or a surrogate mother) and sexual intercourse itself (the couple's natural act may be helped). So that scientists can have the best possibility of ensuring that a fertilised egg will grow successfully when placed in a woman's uterus, usually several eggs are fertilised creating spare embryos which may be stored, destroyed or used for future experimentation. Since, for the Church, life begins at conception, the embryo is to be afforded the same respect given to all human subjects.

Whilst emphasising that a child is not to become the subject of science the document *Donum Vitae* concludes that whatever method is employed to enable a child to be born, once we have human life it is to be respected and loved.

Contraception

Part of the dignity which human beings have is to share in the creative, self-giving nature of God, and the proper context for this is marriage. The making of love through sexual intercourse should express the quality and potential of the married relationship of husband and wife for the giving of life – through enrichment of each other as individuals – and openness to the possibility of having a family.

Couples are called to be responsible in parenthood. When deciding in conscience on the number of children to have, and when to have them, couples are encouraged to use the natural rhythms of the body and practise 'natural family planning'. Artificial methods of birth control are considered not to be fully in keeping with the full expression of sexual love because they deliberately separate the 'unitive' and 'procreative' aspects of sex. (See *Humanae Vitae*, 12). Some oral contraceptives have abortifacient effects as well.

The Salvation Army

Family Planning

Christian marriage has as its divinely ordained end the life-long companionship of husband and wife, hallowed by mutual love for God and each other. Both spiritual fellowship and physical union play their part in this.

However, it is recognised that many married couples will find it necessary to limit the number of their children for various reasons; any such decision, including the contraceptive means to be used, should be taken responsibly and where necessary under medical advice.

Abortion should not be seen as an alternative to contraception.

Abortion

The Salvation Army believes in the sanctity of all human life from the moment of fertilisation. It considers each person to be of infinite value, and each life a gift from God to be cherished, nurtured and preserved.

The Salvation Army actively supports efforts to protect and promote the welfare of the weak and defenceless person, including the unborn. It takes seriously the rights and needs of both the foetus and the mother. It accepts that the termination of a pregnancy may be justified on certain limited grounds; that is, where, in the judgement of competent medical and allied staff, the pregnancy poses a serious threat to the life of the mother, or could result in irreversible physical injury to the mother.

In cases of proven rape or legally defined incest an abortion may be justified because of the extent to which the rape and incest violate the whole person. Termination of a pregnancy may also be justified where reliable diagnostic procedures determine that a foetal abnormality is present which is incompatible with life other than brief post-natal survival or where there is total absence of cognitive function.

In The Salvation Army's experience, where unwanted pregnancies occur, in most instances it is best to counsel acceptance of the situation by all involved, for the foetus to be carried to term, and for all possible supportive help to be given.

When an abortion has taken place The Salvation Army will seek to offer loving and compassionate pastoral care.

A serious commitment to the protection and care of the unborn calls The Salvation Army to promote and work for a society in which all those born into it find loving acceptance and the resources necessary to enable them to reach their fullest potential.

Positional Statements 1 and 2, revised 1992.

In-vitro fertilisation, embryo transfer and artificial insemination

The Salvation Army has no positional statement concerning in-vitro fertilisation, human embryo transfer or AID/AIH. However these areas are subject to ongoing debate with the Army's Moral and Social Issues Council.

In any consideration of the subjects mentioned the following considerations have usually been outlined by way of introduction.

The Christian view of man:

• Human life is a gift from God. Reproduction is the process by which the creative activity of God continues.

• The individual is a unity of body, mind and spirit. These are not considered as components but as dimensions of human existence.

• God loves the individual intimately and specifically.

• Human activity should be directed towards enhancing life and relieving physical and emotional suffering.

Similarly, the following statements concerning Christian behaviour have served to guide discussion:

• The Divine intention for marriage is that it be a loving and life-long union of one man and one woman to the exclusion of all others. This intention is clearly expressed in the Christian Marriage ceremony where the relationship is confirmed by solemn covenant.

• God's will is that sexual union and human reproduction be confined to the marital relation-ship, leading to the establishment of a secure family unit.

- Although children are regarded as the crowning blessing of marriage, a couple's desire for them should never outweigh the mutual obligations of husband and wife to each other.

- The protection and (wherever possible) enhancement of human life are primary concerns over all other considerations. This is well expressed in the compassionate care of the sick, mentally defective, elderly, and dying. It is thought inconsistent not to apply the same principle to the pre-natal stage of development. The Christian does not decide the 'value' of the life requiring care.

The rapidly changing nature of work in the fields of in-vitro fertilisation, embryo transfer and artificial insemination would leave any definitive statement outdated almost as soon as it is made. However there would be acknowledgement that the development of IVF, human embryo transfer and AID are major advances in the treatment of infertility.

Source: Notes prepared for submissions to committees of enquiry both in the UK and Australia (1982–7).

The United Reformed Church

Abortion

The URC has not had major debates about abortion since the 1970s when a study pamphlet was prepared for the churches, setting out some of the issues on which Christians have to make a choice.

A wide range of views remain within the URC, from the few who would want to ban abortion in all but the most exceptional cases to those who believe that women have a right to choose whether to give birth or not. The majority would probably agree that the current limit of 24 weeks is about right, although there would still be some who would argue for a higher or lower limit.

The religious arguments about when life begins are not usually as strongly expressed in discussions within the URC as they would be in, for example, the Roman Catholic Church. Most members of the URC would not want to talk about the foetus as if it were already a child, certainly at an early point in a pregnancy. They would prefer to talk about 'a potential human being' and would see its well-being related to the well-being of the woman nurturing it. The rights of the woman and the rights of the unborn cannot, for most members of the URC, be put on an equal footing because the foetus cannot survive without the woman and, therefore, does not have equal weighting.

No one positively supports abortion as a principle. The debate about any particular abortion would therefore be seen as a debate about the 'lesser of two evils', hinging on the factors to be taken into account in the decision in each case. Many would agree with abortion after rape, when there is the strong risk of handicap or hereditary disease and when the health of the mother would be seriously affected. There would be differences of opinion about the weighting to be given to such factors as the size of the family, the age of the mother, the fact that the woman was married or not, and so on.

Christians are not only concerned with legislation and administration. They realise that individuals who have to take decisions about abortion are often in need of support, encouragement and guidance, for the decision is rarely a simple matter, and social pressures are great. We need to help such people to see the issues and principles involved clearly, and continue to support them in the aftermath of the decision, whatever it may be. We must avoid the danger of being legalistic and condemnatory, for the gospel is concerned with forgiveness and efforts to build a more compassionate, supportive society.

Section 3 • Gender

The Baptist Union of Great Britain

Baptists believe that God created humanity, male and female, in God's own image and in consequence that both sexes reflect something of God's own being.

So far as Christian ministry is concerned, Baptists are concerned to ask whether a person is called and equipped for the task rather than whether they are male or female. There is no necessary reason why the same principle should not be applied to any other kind of work.

Since the 1920s Baptists have been ordaining women to Christian ministry. However, at the beginning of 1994 only about 6% of their accredited ministers were women.

The Church of England

The Church of England affirms the belief that men and women are created in God's image. They are therefore of equal worth in the eyes of God, both reflecting something of his nature. The relationship between men and women should be co-dependent and complementary, characterised by trust and co-operation. This shared status means that men and women should have the same opportunities open to them, though they may choose particular, often complementary, roles.

Whilst these beliefs are affirmed in theory, the Church herself recognises that historically this equality has often not been reflected in her attitudes, and that there are still areas today, for example in her own practice as an employer, in which improvements in attitude are needed. The Church of England also recognises that within society decadent attitudes exist towards women and sexuality and that these are a very real problem, which the Church has a responsibility to challenge.

Women today take an active and significant role in the work of the Church of England. They take part in and lead worship, administer churches and parishes and sit on Parochial Church Councils and on Deanery, Diocesan and General Synods. For many years women have been lay readers and deaconesses. Today they can also be ordained as deacons and as priests. As deacons they can baptise children or adults and can conduct marriage and funeral services. As priests, they can bless the bread and wine for Holy Communion, bless a congregation in God's name and absolve people of their sins. The first ordinations of women priests took place in Bristol Cathedral in March 1994. In the Church of England, women's religious orders were re-established in the 19th century and there are over thirty religious communities in England, for example, the Order of the Holy Paraclete and the Community of St Mary the Virgin.

The Church of Scotland

Women and men play a full and equal part in the Church of Scotland. For over a hundred years women served the Church as deaconesses; now men and women deacons work alongside the ordained ministry. The General Assembly agreed to ordain women as elders in 1966 and as ministers in 1968, but there is still much to be done to ensure that the gifts and ministries of women are used to the full. Inclusiveness should be the mark of the Church.

All of us, male and female, have feminine and masculine potential in more or less random amounts. Gender has to be seen as a spectrum on which we all share degrees of masculinity and femininity, and the worth and dignity of each person on that spectrum should be recognised.

Through stories told by church women, it is apparent that violence against women is a problem within the Church as well as outside it. In Scotland a project was launched called Vashti: Scottish Christian Women Against Abuse. In the Old Testament Book of Esther Vashti refused to be shown off to the people as an object of beauty by her husband, who was drunk at the time. He then dismissed her and gave her royal position to another woman.

The Church has recognised that abuse and violence against women may also be a problem within the families of ministers. This was one of the factors which led to the Board of Ministry arranging for a 24-

hour telephone help-line to be set up for 'Manse families'. This has since been extended to all employees of the Church of Scotland.

Through a 'Gender Attitude Project' (GAP) the Church has tried to educate its members regarding the role of women and men in society to help overcome gender stereotyping and prejudice. The Gender Attitude Project (GAP) explains that it is not enough to change structures; underlying attitudes must also be changed. GAP offers workshops to help people face up to their own attitudes at home, at work and in the Church.

The Methodist Church

A number of reports to the Methodist Conference have recognised that the biological sex of a person is not invariably the same as the gender they feel themselves to be. A person who is biologically 'male' may feel much more comfortable when regarded by others as being of female gender. Their awareness of themselves is that they are primarily female.

Our gender identity seems to be largely determined by our upbringing and the expectations of other people, especially those caring intimately for us. Medically speaking the physical aspects of our sexuality, our genital organs, may be contradictory with how we feel ourselves personally to be. Such people may describe themselves as 'a woman in a man's body'. They may be homosexual rather than heterosexual in their sexual orientation and usually refer to themselves as gay, if a man, or, if a woman, as lesbian. They are attracted for intimate and loving companionship not to members of the opposite sex, but to members of their own sex.

It seems as though human sexuality is in fact a spectrum. Some men feel themselves to be strongly male, others less strongly so. And the same goes for women. Hence the stories about gentle giants and fierce witches. The image of a spectrum suggests that many people are somewhere broadly in the middle, being exclusively neither male nor female in their attitudes, however obviously male or female their biological make-up may be. It seems as though between 0.5% and 5% of the population may have a gender orientation that differs from their sexual biology.

Just as with heterosexual people, some homosexual people remain celibate: they do not engage in genital 'acts of sex' with another person. They express their love through friendship, and through physical contact which falls short of genital union.

Sometimes gays or lesbians need very sympathetic help in adjusting to their situation, including counselling and even, in rare cases, surgery. In other cases people are content with their situation and proud of who they are. They feel they were 'born gay'. They look not for sympathy, but for acceptance.

The response of Methodism is dealt with in Section 4: Homosexuality.

Basis: *Human Sexuality*, a report to the Methodist Conference 1990.

The Russian Orthodox Church

Equal rights

A modern writer has pointed out that it was Christianity which recognised the fundamental equality of the sexes before God in his teaching. Orthodox Christian doctrine permits no qualitative differentiation between men and women in their essential humanity. Women, according to Orthodox Christian beliefs, may not be considered inferior beings and must be accorded rights due to every human being. Thus any laws, practices, prejudices, social or cultural traditions which deny to women life, dignity, liberty, basic needs and equal access to them are to be condemned as unchristian.

Woman's rights

Women and men are equal but important differences are also present. There are significant and important roles in the Church and in society which are unique to women. This is based on women's God-given role and task as mother. Nothing in any equal rights campaign should undermine the high privilege, dignity and honour which women alone have to give birth to, nurture and morally and spiritually guide future generations. No employment, however lucrative, powerful, influential or creative can supersede in value the conscientious and responsible giving of life and nurture to a human being. When the mother is a Christian who co-operates with God in the making of new human beings and incorporating them into the Kingdom of God through his Church, there is no greater dignity and honour. Women are due equal rights as persons – yet their special role and calling transcends such legal formulations. The Orthodox Church opposes those who would minimise, denigrate and weaken the unique and lofty calling of women in their roles as wives, mothers, and home makers. In all this, the special and exemplary role of Our Most Holy Lady Mary Mother of God and ever pure Virgin is held central in Orthodox teaching.

The Religious Society of Friends (Quakers)

The ministry of women

Since Quakers believe in the 'priesthood of all believers' they do not have an ordained clergy. The ordination of women is therefore not an issue for them in the way that it is in some other churches.

Quakers believe that every person is potentially capable of understanding the will of God, and helping others to reach God. We see one of the tasks of a church as being to help individuals develop this inherent gift – or as George Fox put it, to reach towards 'that of God in everyone'. This is true of women, men, children and adults, so in our silent worship anyone who feels moved to speak may do so, and in our business meetings any member may hold office.

To be without an ordained clergy is not to be without leadership or ministry. People are appointed to particular tasks, usually for a limited period of time. Quakers look for gifts and talents and skills, and recognise that as people grow and change, different gifts may develop.

Since the beginning of our history, Quaker women have preached, taught, travelled in the ministry and given spiritual leadership and guidance equally with men. In the seventeenth century, however, men and women were seen to have different kinds of talents, roles and tasks, and therefore women's business meetings were set up to fulfil separate jobs (particularly pastoral care). For over a century these self-determining women's business meetings were held, giving women experience in running organisations which some of them used to good effect in leading the early anti-slavery and feminist movements.

Women and men in the Society of Friends united in business meetings in the mid-nineteenth century. In the twentieth century we have had several examples of women serving the Yearly Meeting as Clerk. The

first woman appointed to be Clerk was W Maude Brayshaw in 1943. The current (1999) Clerks of both Yearly Meeting and Meeting for Sufferings are female.

Whilst equality in all business and organisational matters has been the principle, until recently there was a tendency in the Society of Friends for more men to be Treasurers and more women to be concerned with Pastoral Care. In this they reflected the kind of stereotypical thinking of the wider society in which they live. Within the Quaker movement in Britain today there is a deep concern to redress the balance by actively seeking men and women for all tasks. Sexist language is also something that we are very wary of. In the revision of our Book of Discipline which has just taken place, inclusive language has been used and a wider range of contributions from women has been included.

The Roman Catholic Church

Sexuality is a fundamental part of what it is to be a human person created male or female and loved by God. The Church teaches that men and women are equals, co-stewards of creation. They were 'made for each other', called to be a 'communion of persons', and are 'complementary as masculine and feminine'. The *Catechism of the Catholic Church* expresses this well when it states:

> Each of the two sexes is an image of the power and tenderness of God, with equal dignity though in a different way. (CCC §2335)

Friendship is greatly valued – whether between members of the opposite or the same sex.

The Salvation Army

Female ministry

From its foundation in 1865, The Salvation Army has accepted women on equal terms with men in all aspects of ministry.

The scriptural justification for this was forcibly argued by Catherine Booth (who, with her husband William, was co-founder of the movement) in a pamphlet entitled *Female Ministry*, which was published in the late 1850s; she herself first spoke from the pulpit at Gateshead in 1860.

Of the 91 full-time officers exercising spiritual and administrative leadership in local corps (churches) in 1878, 41 were women. Women did pioneering work in a number of countries. Today world-wide, women account for more than half of the ordained officers of The Salvation Army.

The principle of equality has had its critics – one of the reasons for the historic decision not to administer the Eucharist in Salvation Army meetings was that some would not accept the validity of that priestly function being performed by women – but it has proved its worth in practice. No position of authority (temporal or spiritual) is reserved for men – the offices of divisional commander and territorial commander can be occupied by women officers, and two of its Generals (international leaders) have been women.

The United Reformed Church

Equal opportunities

In 1994 Assembly adopted an Equal Opportunity Policy as follows:

(a) The Church affirms in its *Basis of Union* that 'all ministries shall be open to both men and women'. At Assembly 1987 it adopted a Declaration on Racism and in 1990 adopted a Declaration of Equal Opportunities Policy in relation to ministers.

(b) This policy is not a statement of what the Church has already achieved; it is a declaration of the way it intends to move forward at all levels and in all aspects of its life within the limitations of its resources. In particular, it is an aid to appointing the most suitable people to all positions of responsibility within the church disregarding irrelevant considerations; it does not oblige the church as employer or otherwise to make

appointments of people other than those most capable of fulfilling the responsibilities.

Assembly declared:

(i) The Church will behave as an 'equal opportunities organisation' and not discriminate on grounds of race, gender or disability.

(ii) The Church works to combat racism, sexism and prejudice against people with disabilities and is committed to positive action rather than containing the issues.

(iii) The Church is aware of possible barriers, for example to women, black people and people with disabilities, within the structures of the Church, in ministry and other posts; this has to do with expectations, position, role and status.

(iv The Church will therefore establish appropriate methods of monitoring the appointment, call, representation and position of women, black people and people with disabilities in the Church and take appropriate action where necessary.

Assembly resolved to appoint a Standing Committee of people with experience of Equal Opportunities, including two representatives of each category covered by the policy. The terms of reference are:

a   To develop detailed equal opportunities policies.

b   To have oversight of training programmes in equal opportunities.

c   To monitor the implementation of the equal opportunity policy.

d   To report annually to the General Assembly on the implementation of the policy.

Section 4 • Homosexuality

The Baptist Union of Great Britain

The Baptist Union Assembly has not issued a statement about this. However, a policy does exist with regard to ministers. Certain forms of conduct are regarded as 'unbecoming' to a person called to ministry. With respect to homosexuality, the following guidelines have been approved:

> Homosexual orientation (whether male or female) is not of itself a reason for exclusion from ministry, but homosexual genital practice is to be regarded as unacceptable in the pastoral office, and is to be treated as falling within these guidelines. Ministers are expected not to advocate homosexual or lesbian genital relationships as acceptable alternatives to male/female partnership in marriage.

The Church of England

The Church of England, like other Churches and the wider society, has found the issue of homosexuality difficult to discuss. It is part of a broader debate on human sexuality and should be considered within this context.

In 1987, the General Synod affirmed that the biblical and traditional teaching on chastity and fidelity in personal relationships is a response to, and expression of God's love for each one of us. In particular, it affirmed

1 that sexual intercourse is an act of total commitment which belongs properly within a permanent married relationship;

2 that fornication and adultery are sins against this ideal and are to be met by a call to repentance and the exercise of compassion;

3 that homosexual genital acts also fall short of this ideal and are likewise to be met by a call to repentance and the exercise of compassion;

4 that all Christians are called to be exemplary in all spheres of morality, including sexual morality and that holiness of life is particularly required of Christian Leaders.

In December 1991, the Bishops of the Church of England published *Issues in Human Sexuality*, which examined issues related to homosexuality in the context of human sexuality as a whole. It treated human sexuality in a very positive way. The bishops emphasised that Christians must reject all forms of hatred towards homosexual people; they should protect those who are victimised. The report was honest, too, in its recognition that Christians are divided in their view of homosexuality. Many of these differences of opinion arise from different interpretations of various passages of scripture. The report urged caution, in particular, in the interpretation of Old Testament passages. The Church has always drawn a distinction between ritual and moral laws, and the status and meaning of the laws which could refer to homosexuality are open to question. It called for congregations to be places where all can live in fellowship and affirmed that homosexual people are in every way as valuable and as valued by God as heterosexual people. It emphasised the need for Christians to listen to those who can speak relevantly from personal experience. The report ended by stating: 'If we are faithful to Our Lord, then disagreement over the proper expression of homosexual love will never become rejection of the homosexual person.'

The need for ongoing discussion is recognised and the Church of England urges prayerful study and reflection by its clergy and congregations on these matters.

The Church of Scotland

The Bible does not offer us a set of detailed rules regarding sexual behaviour, but an account of God's relationship with his people. Our sexuality is both a divine gift and a human responsibility. We have to apply the insights of scripture with regard to our sexuality to our contemporary knowledge and experience. In the light of God's unconditional love the context of the full physical expression of all our relationships will be a mutual self-giving love. Celibacy need not be seen as the highest expression of faith and holiness.

Sexuality can be expressed in a variety of loving relationships and creative activities. Genital sexual activity is not the only means of expression. In a culture which has over-eroticised relationships, the Church can help redress the balance by reaffirming the rich blessings that can be experienced in friendships with members of either sex.

Homosexuality includes same-sex attraction on the part of both men and women. Such attraction may include the desire for genital satisfaction, but may be expressed in other ways too. Since sexuality is one of God's gifts and is an essential part of a person's identity, we have to ask whether those with a homosexual orientation should not also be free to express their sexuality.

In Bible passages where homosexual acts are referred to we have to consider how far the material is socially and culturally conditioned.

There is a great deal of prejudice against homosexual people. While there undoubtedly is criminal exploitation and pornography in some homosexual circles, it is wrong always to link homosexual practice with child abuse and paedophilia.

Many within the church believe that sex education should be approached in a way that the appreciation of the value and importance of marriage does not diminish the worth of other loving relationships. The intrinsic worth or moral superiority of any relationship does not depend on any ceremony, religious or secular, but on the way people treat and regard each other in that relationship. It should be part of religious and moral education to encourage young people to reflect on moral values and to learn about and so learn from the beliefs on marriage, family, and sexual relationships held by different world faith communities and even by different denominations or groups within these communities.

Within the Church of Scotland there are divergent opinions regarding 'same sex relationships'. Christians in good faith hold diverse interpretations of God's will in the area of sexual ethics. Between 1993 and 2000 Reports to the General Assembly of the Church of Scotland have contained statements like these which illustrate the variety of standpoints:

• Schools should cover the whole range of sexual orientation sensitively within a developed programme of sex education. It is important for

children to think about the essential qualities of alternatives to marriage since most of them will already be familiar with their existence.

• The institution of marriage is the gift of God to his human creatures. It is the normative context of the deepest and most joyful relationship between a man and a woman, enhanced for Christian partners by their shared faith and their perception of God as the source of all love.

• The practise of homosexual acts is contrary to God's will for humankind.

• Love, trust, forgiveness and faithfulness are the most significant criteria by which all relationships are to be assessed.

• Sexuality is a blessing and gift from God to be experienced and enjoyed without shame or guilt.

• Marriage is appointed as the right and proper setting for the full expression of physical love between man and woman.

The Methodist Church

At its annual Conference in 1993, following long debate at all levels of the Church's life on the basis of a detailed report, the Methodist Church considered the issue of homosexuality (see the Section 3: Gender for the meaning and use of this word). At the end of the debate, the judgement of the annual Conference was passed in the form of resolutions

affirming the joy of human sexuality as God's gift;

condemning all practices of sexuality which are promiscuous, exploitative or demeaning;

stating that no one is to be debarred from the Church on the grounds of sexual orientation in itself;

reaffirming 'the traditional teaching of the Church on human sexuality, namely chastity for all outside marriage and fidelity within it'.

The significance of the last of these resolutions, which was passed by 293 votes to 250, with 16 neutral, lies in the distinction between homosexual 'orientation'

and homosexual 'practices' referred to in the section on Gender. What it means is that while, in the words of another resolution, passed by 313 votes to 217, with 27 neutral, the Methodist Church 'recognises, affirms and celebrates the participation and ministry of lesbians and gay men in the Church', it does not consider that homosexual genital practice, by either Ministers or lay members is acceptable.

Basis: *Human Sexuality*, a report to the Methodist Conference, 1990; *President's Letter to the Methodist People*, June 1993

The Russian Orthodox Church

The Orthodox church has long had a clear and firmly articulated position regarding homosexual acts. It has not had a clear position on homosexuality as a condition since the distinction between homosexual acts and the homosexual condition is the result of recent developments in scientific knowledge.

Regarding homosexual acts, the traditional and exclusive teaching of the church is condemnatory, seeing such acts as morally wrong. The evidence from the sources of the faith, Old Testament, New Testament and patristic teaching, without exception, support this position. Hence, the Church teaches that the only proper place for the exercise of sexual function is in marriage.

The distinction made between the homosexual condition and homosexual acts addresses the pastoral concerns of the Church for persons who are subject to 'exclusive psychosexual attraction towards members of the same sex' (definition of homosexuality from *Encyclopaedia of Bio Ethics*, Volume II, page 671). In the language of the church, this is a 'passion'. It is a wrongful orientation of our desires. (Passions are of many kinds, pride, greed, gluttony, lust, theft, and so on). When such passions exist, no matter how strongly felt, the Church counsels spiritual and moral struggle against them. In our commonly shared struggle against sin in whatever form, the Orthodox Church sees all persons working to fight temptation and overcome passions. Towards this end, the Church offers a panoply of spiritual weapons. These include prayer, worship, fasting, the sacrament of holy confession, reading of scripture and of patristic and spiritual writings, Christian fellowship as well as pastoral and psychotherapeutic counselling. It should also be remembered that we come to Christ, just as

we are, but the threshold of his kingdom is the gate of repentance and the process with which we progress is metanoia – a complete turnabout – towards the will of God from whom grace and wholeness flows.

The following affirmations were made at the 10th All American Council of the Orthodox Church of America in July, 1992.

Homosexuality is to be approached as the result of humanity's rebellion against God, and so against its own nature and well-being. It is not to be taken as a way of living and acting for men and women made in God's image and likeness.

Men and women with homosexual feelings and emotions are to be treated with the understanding, acceptance, love, justice and mercy due to all human beings.

People with homosexual tendencies are to be helped to admit these feelings to themselves and to others who will not reject or harm them. They are to seek assistance in discovering the specific causes of their homosexual orientation, and to work toward overcoming its harmful effects in their lives.

Persons struggling with homosexuality who accept the Orthodox faith and strive to fulfil the Orthodox way of life may be communicants of the Church with everyone else who believes and struggles with temptation.

The Religious Society of Friends (Quakers)

We learn about God though God's indwelling spirit, through the witness of those who have gone before us, and through our human relationships – our love for others and their love for us. We believe that we can know this experimentally (i.e., through experience). This knowledge helps us to 'take heed to the promptings of love and truth in our hearts which are the leadings of God.'

Advices and Queries, 1995

Special friendships may develop into longer-lasting partnerships; the sharing and commitment helping to deepen the loving, joyful, relationship. As such relationships grow (whether they be with someone of the same sex or of the opposite sex), we learn – sometimes painfully – that love gives freedom for each partner to develop as an individual. It does not exploit weaknesses, but always encourages.

Love is affection and friendship; caring and sharing; creative and joyful: giving, receiving and forgiving. It is the acceptance of all aspects of our nature, including our creativity, our intellect, our various faults and abilities, our colour, our sex and our sexuality. When we learn how to love, we learn also how to worship

---

The Recognition of Same-Sex Relationships

This statement, finding the quality of love in relationships rather than sexual orientation, reflects the attitude prevalent among most Quakers in Yearly Meeting, the body which unites Quakers in England, Scotland and Wales. Quakers do not formulate their beliefs in a creed, but a general attitude and common beliefs can be discerned. Some Quakers, however, do have misgivings over the subject of homosexuality.

Most British Quakers, while finding much inspiration in the Bible, would not use it as the final or only authority. They believe in obedience to God's indwelling spirit, tested by the leadings of the larger Quaker community. They tend to be an accepting group of people celebrating diversity.

There have been one or two blessings of same-sex relationships among British Friends, though the marriage regulations assume that marriage is heterosexual. Quite a number of Quakers are openly lesbian, gay, and bisexual.

The Roman Catholic Church

Cardinal Hume in 'A Note on the teaching of the Catholic Church concerning Homosexual People' (Briefing, 16 March 1995, page 4) wrote:

It is necessary to distinguish between sexual orientation or inclination, and engaging in sexual (genital) activity, heterosexual or homosexual. Neither a homosexual nor a heterosexual orientation leads inevitably to sexual activity. Furthermore, an individual's sexual orientation can be unclear, even complex. Also, it may vary over the years. Being a homosexual person is, then, neither morally good nor

morally bad: it is homosexual genital acts that are morally wrong ... The Church does not consider the whole personality and character of the individual to be thereby disordered. Homosexual people, as well as heterosexual people can, and often do, give a fine example of friendship and the art of chaste loving.

Friendship is a gift from God. Friendship is a way of loving. Friendship is necessary for every person. To equate friendship and full sexual involvement with another is to distort the very concept of friendship. Sexual loving presupposes friendship but friendship does not require full sexual involvement. It is a mistake to say or think or presume that if two persons of the same or different sexes enjoy a deep and lasting friendship then they must be sexually involved.

The Salvation Army

The Salvation Army believes that homosexuality can be properly considered only in the broader context of a biblical understanding of human sexuality in general. The creation account set out in the opening chapters of Genesis reveals the following truths:

a That mankind is made in the image of God (Genesis 1:27);

b That God created us both male and female (Genesis 1:27);

c That this differentiation of the sexes is a part of the divine image in the human race (Genesis 1:27);

d That the loneliness of Adam was remedied by God through the creation of a woman, not a second man (Genesis 2:21–22);

e That sexual union leading to a one-flesh relationship is intended to be between male and female (Genesis 2:23–24);

f That such union is intended to be in the setting of a permanent and publicly acknowledged relationship forming the basis of a new family unit (Genesis 2:24).

The Bible thus teaches that God's intention for mankind is that society should be ordered on the basis of lifelong, legally sanctioned heterosexual unions. Such unions (marriages) lead to the formation of social units (families) which are essential to human personal development and therefore to the stability of the community.

Scripture opposes homosexual practices by direct comment (Leviticus 18:22; 20:13; Romans 1:26–27; 1 Corinthians 6:9; 1 Timothy 1:10) and also by clearly implied disapproval (Genesis 19:1–29; Judges 19:1–30; 2 Peter 2:1–22; Jude 3–23). The Bible treats such practices as self-evidently abnormal. They reject both the obvious implications of human physiology and the potential for procreation. Romans 1 sees homosexual acts as a symptom of a deeper refusal to accept the organising scheme of God for the created order (Romans 1:24–25).

The Army recognises that same-sex friendships can be enriching, Christ-honouring relationships, bringing joy through mutual companionship and sharing. However, same-sex relationships which are genitally expressed are unacceptable according to the teaching of scripture. Attempts to establish or promote such relationships as viable alternatives to a heterosexually based family life do not conform to God's will for society.

The Army is opposed to the victimisation of persons on the grounds of sexual orientation and recognises the social and emotional stress and the loneliness borne by many who are homosexual.

The Army regards the origins of a homosexual orientation as a mystery and does not regard a homosexual disposition as blameworthy in itself or rectifiable at will. Nevertheless, whilst we are not responsible for what we are, we are accountable for what we do; and homosexual conduct, like heterosexual conduct, is controllable and may be morally evaluated therefore in the light of scriptural teaching.

However, it believes firmly in the power of God's grace to enable the maintenance of a life-style pleasing to him, including a life-style built upon celibacy and self-restraint for those who will not or cannot marry.

No one who yields to the lordship of Christ and who undertakes by his grace to live in accordance with the teaching of scripture is excluded from Christian fellowship and service in the Army.

Positional Statement 8, revised January 1992.

The United Reformed Church

The United Reformed Church published in 1991 a document with the title *Homosexuality: a Christian View*. It is the product of a working party established by the Church and Society Department but the views expressed are those of the working party only.

The report consists of a relatively short main statement with considerably longer background papers by two members of the group on 'Homosexuality and the Bible' and 'A Medical View of Homosexuality', and fourteen extracts from letters received by the working party during the course of its deliberations. There is also an interesting bibliography of novels, short stories and case histories offering insights into homosexual relationships. The article on 'Homosexuality and the Bible' is a scholarly presentation of the argument for regarding the biblical passages on homosexuality as culturally conditioned, and therefore of limited applicability to the modern world.

Heterosexual Christians must ask themselves whether and on what grounds those of homosexual orientation are to be denied the joy of sexual expression.

The Working Party acknowledges that the text of the Bible, when it mentions homosexual behaviour at all, does so in condemnatory terms, though the actual references are few and it is not always clear what the precise understanding of the writers was. The question is whether the apparent teaching on homosexuality belongs to an era beyond which we have come or whether it is part of that 'core of belief' without which no authentic community of faith can live.

In short, the Working Party is not prepared to describe homosexual activity as intrinsically sinful in principle, though any sexual activity is easily spoiled by pride, greed, lust or other forms of selfishness.

A second volume has been published by the Group for Evangelism and Renewal within the United Reformed Church called *Homosexuality and the Gospel*. This challenges the basic premise of the first document:

> We believe that the great majority of Christians still hold, with us, the view that all genital sexual acts outside of marriage, including homosexual acts, are sinful and are not within the intention of God. Therefore, if any seek to establish another standard

for Christian sexual morality, the burden of proof must rest upon them.

We also believe that the Bible's teaching is quite plain and has not been negated by modern scholarship.

This document makes a clear distinction between homosexual orientation and practice and admits that homosexual people are not always welcomed in Christian congregations:

Christians need to abandon their phobias about homosexuality and offer homosexual people the love and support they need to fulfil God's calling for them.

The document then sets out some objectives for a local church in five areas: education, challenge, counselling, discipline and support. It too includes a number of personal testimonies.

The United Reformed Church published a third volume in 1995 entitled *Speaking for Ourselves*. This is an anthology of personal stories and affirmations. The Assembly in 1995 launched an extended period of discussion of these matters in the Church with a view to further debate at the Assembly in 1997.

Section 5 • Substance Abuse

The Baptist Union of Great Britain

Baptists are concerned with the abuse of substances and have traditionally adopted an abstinence approach. The complexity of life has led to a more liberal approach to the use of substances. Many Baptists today will experiment with alcohol and tobacco, although the majority of Baptists would promote moderate use of such drugs. Baptists are influenced by the words of St Paul who reminds us that we ourselves are God's temple.

Alcohol

The abuse of drugs is not a new problem for our society. Alcohol has been seen as a major social problem for society for the last 200 years. The abuse of alcohol leads to premature death, and alcoholism has led to the break up of many families. The level at which alcohol becomes a problem is still debated by the medical profession, but there are safety levels as defined by the Department of Health that can be of help.

Tobacco

Tobacco has also been seen as a drug that many Baptists are concerned about. Its abuse again has very serious health implications. The dangers of passive smoking were highlighted by the sad death of Roy Castle, a member of the Baptist family.

Illegal drugs

Illegal drug misuse has emerged as a major problem, and a response has been sought by a number of Baptists. The traditional approach of 'Just say No' is not seen as a helpful tool in providing drugs education to protect young people. The response from the Baptist community is a more mature response that grapples with the complexities that are involved with substance abuse.

This view is able to take seriously the desire of people to experiment with substances. The abuse of substances is normally symptomatic of other circumstances such as abuse, a sense of not coping, poor social and economic situation.

Baptists are concerned with people taking illegal drugs, and do not condone this in any way. This view does not mean that all Baptists agree with current policies pertaining to certain drugs. The common view is that other drugs such as cannabis should not be legalised although there are significant voices amongst the Baptist family that believe a review of policy through a Royal Commission is required.

Baptists also are opposed to a war on drugs, because it has been found that this in reality leads to a war on the victims of drug abuse. Someone who has a drug misuse problem is still one of God's children and worthy of respect. Drug users who need help with their drug problem are encouraged to seek it, and there are a number of agencies that are Christian-based that can provide support in numerous ways.

Baptists believe that their faith is central to their lives, and gives them the support and confidence to face their lives. Drug abuse is symptomatic of the consequences of life without the knowledge of God that can lead to a search for meaning and a sense of false confidence that certain drugs can create.

The Church of England

The Church of England sees the whole issue of drug abuse as having its roots in those feelings of disaffection which can exist in a strongly materialistic, individualistic and consumer-orientated society. The Church has a long history of working alongside people who abuse alcohol and drugs. It tries to promote social conditions which allow people to live with dignity without turning to alcohol or illegal drugs. It also tries to encourage that sense of self-confidence in individuals, which will help them resist the pressures of a drug-taking society.

The Church recognises that it is faced with the challenge of a youth culture which in many ways is far removed from Church life. It also acknowledges the continuing growth in drug use by many young people, including those in Church congregations.

The General Synod, in a recent debate, deplored the destructive effects of drugs on individuals and communities. The Church of England's concern is to support efforts to tackle drug misuse, to address the issue of education as a means of prevention, as well as giving practical help to those individuals and communities whose lives are blighted by drugs. A General Synod motion called for more resources to be spent on drug education and commended those who worked in drug rehabilitation.

The drinking of alcohol, but not drunkenness, is affirmed in scripture. There are those who advocate abstinence, while others seek to offer an example of moderation and self-control. The Church of England encourages individual Christians to be informed about the arguments for each position, to make up their own mind on these matters, and to respect the views of others. The Church does not then advocate abstinence herself, but calls for moderate drinking, and points to the effect of drunkenness in marital violence and crime.

The Church of Scotland

Alcohol

While the Church of Scotland has traditionally taken the view that the Christian's attitude to alcohol should be either total abstinence or moderation, it is concerned that for so many today alcohol is seen as an essential ingredient to life. There needs to be a fundamental change in attitude to the place of alcohol in our society. One way of controlling the abuse of alcohol would be by raising the price. The Church favours a reduction in the legal blood alcohol level for all drivers. Concern about the steady rise in under-age drinking has led the Church to challenge the use of football strips and sports clothing (especially children's clothing) as a means of advertising alcohol. The Church has viewed with concern the introduction of 'Alcoholic Lemonade' and other alcoholic designer drinks which look and taste like soft drinks and which are targeted at young people.

Smoking

The Church regards smoking as a health hazard and has recommended that smoking should be banned on Church premises. It has expressed regret that as smoking declines in the developed countries, the tobacco industry is transferring more and more resources to the developing countries.

Drugs

For over thirty years the Church of Scotland has been calling on its members to recognise the pernicious effects of drug addiction and solvent abuse and to exercise caution in the use of all habit-forming drugs. Taking risks with drugs should be as socially unacceptable as taking risks with the consumption of alcohol. The deepest needs of society cannot be met apart from God and the life which Jesus Christ offers.

The Methodist Church

Drugs are part of creation. Some are produced by natural means, others manufactured by chemical processes. The human mind which has developed these processes is also part of creation. God has offered these gifts and expects human beings to exercise responsibility and stewardship in their use. They should be employed in ways which promote health and healing. Many people are living full and active lives who, but for medically prescribed drugs, would be incapacitated or dead.

Very large numbers of young people find recreation and excitement in using illicit drugs. A small minority become drug dependent. Our concern is to reduce the harm and havoc that such drug use can cause.

The effect on health of different substances (including tobacco and alcohol) varies enormously. The Methodist Church should do everything it can to encourage well-informed, open debate. The agenda will include:

what constitutes healthy living;

information about drugs of all kinds, and the skill of differentiating between them;

the frequent mismatch between what we know and how we behave (for example smoking in spite of the known health hazards);

the impact of social conditions on health and behaviour.

There is a special concentration on family life and support for communities and groups in the Church's work. This will be important, in partnership with other agencies, in fostering healthy life-styles in society, building self-confidence and self-esteem in young and old, and enabling young people to capture a vision of a drug-free life.

The Church, when inspired by God's Spirit, offers hospitality, affirmation and respect to the damaged, deprived, drug-dependent and broken people of our society. Judgemental attitudes are wholly inappropriate. Refuge, support, patience and hopefulness are fundamental elements in the Church's ministry.

Alcohol

Methodism has been closely associated in many people's minds with total abstinence from alcohol. The Church has always highlighted the dangers of dependency on alcohol and the damage it causes to personal well-being and social relationships. The judgement of the Methodist Church, however, is that total abstinence is a matter for individual choice. It is not a condition of membership. Methodists are recommended to make a personal commitment either to total abstinence or to responsible drinking.

The Methodist Church has an honourable tradition of direct contact with and ministry to men and women who are alcohol dependent. Its members have offered support to them in many ways.

Basis: *The Non-Medical Use of Drugs*, A Declaration of the Methodist Church 1974; *Through a Glass Darkly: Responsible Attitudes to Alcohol*, 1987; *Substances of Abuse: Getting a Perspective*, 1995.

The Religious Society of Friends (Quakers)

Quakers are concerned with conscience, social responsibility, health, and sensitivity to God, self, and other people. Any decision the individual makes on the issue of substance abuse needs to take all these concerns into account. The statement in *Quaker Faith and Practice* encourages prudence:

> Many yearly meetings hold very strong testimonies against any use of tobacco or alcohol. Within Britain Yearly Meeting some Friends advocate total abstinence from alcohol, others counsel moderation. Those who smoke tobacco, drink alcohol or abuse other substances risk damage to their own health and may hurt or endanger other people. Such use can deaden a person's sensitivity and response to others and to

God. Consider whether you should avoid these products altogether, discourage their use in others, especially young people, and refrain from any share in their manufacture or sale. Maintain your own integrity and do not let social pressures influence your decisions.

Quaker Faith and Practice 20:40, 1995

The Salvation Army

Addictive drugs

The Salvation Army accepts that many drugs beneficial to health can produce addiction. Only the physician can weigh the advantages and the risks of prescribing for each patient.

The deliberate misuse of such drugs to induce oblivion or hallucinatory states is condemned. The physical, mental and emotional disturbances due to such misuse are well known to The Salvation Army, which will continue to offer treatment to the victims of addiction, realising that such practices stem from deep emotional and spiritual problems and are especially common in young persons.

Alcohol

The most common drug of addiction is alcohol. The Salvation Army, recognising both spiritual and temporal dangers inherent in the use of alcoholic drinks, has always required total abstinence of its soldiers. While not condemning those outside its ranks who choose to indulge, it nevertheless believes total abstinence to be the only certain guarantee against over-indulgence and the evils of addiction.

Experience has shown a direct connection between the incidence of addiction and the easy availability of alcoholic drinks together with the increasing social acceptance of their consumption. The Salvation Army actively supports legislation likely to reduce the consumption of alcohol.

Social drinking

The easy availability of alcohol and its inclusion at social functions has led to more frequent invitations for the abstainer to take alcohol. Although an occasional social drink does not inevitably lead to alcoholism, alcohol impairs judgement and is a contributory factor in many social tragedies. Salvationists, whose work brings them into contact with the victims of such tragedies, believe that abstinence is the most effective way to set an example of personal responsibility in their private lives.

Tobacco

Tobacco is a narcotic, whose use, in all forms that tobacco can be used, has always been discouraged by

The Salvation Army. Since 1975 complete abstinence from tobacco has been required of Salvationists.

The Salvation Army accepts the evidence presented by medical science of the effects of tobacco on the body and believes that the Bible (1 Corinthians 6:19–20) supports the acceptance of this discipline.

Positional Statement, 1992.

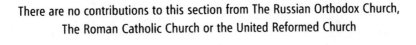

There are no contributions to this section from The Russian Orthodox Church,
The Roman Catholic Church or the United Reformed Church

Section 6 • The End of Life

The Baptist Union of Great Britain

The questions raised by euthanasia are similar in many ways to those raised by abortion. In principle, Baptists are opposed to it because life is God's gift and because any relationship is worth preserving, however poor or shallow it may be.

However, where a person is 'brain-dead' and incapable of establishing or maintaining a relationship of any kind and where the relatives and friends concerned feel that any relationship has ceased and where medical opinion is that no recovery is possible, most Baptists accept that it is not wrong for treatment to be withdrawn and thus for the patient to be allowed to die.

The Church of England

The biblical and theological principles that underpin the Church of England's views on issues of ageing, euthanasia and suicide relate to the concepts of the sanctity of human life and the limits of human autonomy.

Older people

As we live longer, the number of older people in our society increases. The Church of England sees its role in paying attention to the needs of older people, and to the needs of those who care for them. Older people can often feel undervalued and the Church seeks to both celebrate and support their prayer, work and witness in its life.

Suicide

Traditionally the Christian Churches were very severe on suicides and attempted suicides, refusing the former burial in consecrated ground. Suicide was an expression of a total lack of faith in God. Nowadays, Christians generally recognise that suicide is not so much a deliberate rejection of life as an expression of dissatisfaction with the particular life the person is leading, and in many cases a cry for help. Seeing things in this way has led Christians to seek to help potential suicides, where possible, and certainly not to engage in moral condemnation of them. The Church was responsible for pressing the Government to de-criminalise suicide in 1961.

Euthanasia

Human life is a gift from God to be preserved and nourished. It is a Christian imperative to offer protection and special care to those who become vulnerable through illness or disability. The Church of England is resolutely opposed to the legalisation of euthanasia even though others may argue that it is a means of relieving suffering, shortening the anguish of families or friends, or saving scarce resources. It believes that the interests of the vulnerable must be protected, even if this means limiting the freedom of others to determine their end.

A distinction is made between killing and letting someone die. Whilst to accede to requests for voluntary euthanasia would be wrong, doctors do not have an overriding obligation to prolong life by all available means, if to do so is also to prolong suffering. The primary duties of doctors, as protectors of life, are to ensure that patients are as free from pain as possible, enabled to make informed choices about their future lives, and supported through the personal challenges which face them. There are limits to human autonomy, to what human beings may do to themselves or require others to do for them. The actions of individuals can have social consequences. If euthanasia were allowed, the value of human life would be undermined.

The hospice movement is commended as a positive alternative, enabling people to be helped to die with dignity. This work has enriched not only the lives of the terminally ill, but also those around them.

The Church of Scotland

Euthanasia and suicide

The Church of Scotland believes that Christians have no right to dispose of their own lives. However those who commit or attempt to commit suicide should be treated with compassion and understanding rather than with condemnation. Aiding or abetting suicide is illegal in Scotland.

There can be no support for terminating someone's life even when that is requested. The fundamental principle is that of the sanctity of human life. Our individual worth does not depend on ability or gifts or the quality of our life but upon our status as beings made in God's image.

The Church takes euthanasia to mean deliberately terminating the life of another person in the context of terminal, painful or distressing illness. Where a doctor knowingly injects a lethal dose of a drug into a patient even for humane and caring reasons it is still wrong. However where a doctor decides that further treatment is futile and not in the best interests of the patient, or where the proposed treatment needed for the relief of pain is given in the knowledge that it may at the same time shorten the patient's expectation of life, such actions should not be regarded as euthanasia.

The Voluntary Euthanasia Society of Scotland stresses the emphasis on voluntary and on termination on compassionate grounds. However the Church believes that the VESS does not take enough account of how its proposals might be abused, what effect they might have on those who have to facilitate the termination, or how, were legislation to be passed to allow euthanasia, other sick people might be made to feel vulnerable.

Some organisations favour the drawing up of a 'living will' whereby an individual lays down instructions as to healthcare and treatment to be applied in the event of his or her incapacity. But in a living will one cannot insist that a doctor or anyone else, should put the will-maker to death.

The Church opposes the legalising of euthanasia. Instead it believes more attention should be paid to alternatives. It commends the further development of palliative medicine and hospice care and encourages Christians to give all support and assistance to these and other life-affirming alternatives to the deliberate termination of life in the context of serious illness.

The Methodist Church

Nowadays euthanasia has the special sense of taking deliberate steps to end human life, usually with the intention of avoiding extreme pain, distress or helplessness. The Methodist Church is strongly opposed to euthanasia.

This opposition is partly based on the practical difficulties that would be faced by doctors and other medical staff. Who would make the decisions? What would the impact be on staff working in the hospital of knowing that euthanasia was administered there? Would relatives be encouraged to be present … as loved ones, as witnesses? These practical problems, and their implications for relationships between professional staff, patients and close relatives are obvious. The medical profession as a whole is opposed to legalising of euthanasia.

There is also the difficulty of framing legislation in such a way as to exclude its misuse in the shape of allowing 'difficult' patients to be done away with, allowing relatives to short circuit the natural life span of a difficult individual.

A firm conviction against euthanasia does not lessen the complex moral problems integral to the final stages of some terminal illnesses. Sometimes, for example, the management of excessive pain may have the outcome of shortening life. On other occasions it may be extremely difficult to ascertain in what sense, if any, a patient may be judged still to be alive (for example, persistent vegetative state).

One of the issues being examined in a current Methodist study is that of 'living wills'. This is an indication by the author of what would be a legal document that he or she does not wish, should they become ill with no apparent hope of recovery, to be 'kept alive'. In other words, once that stage is reached, no further treatment would be given except to relieve pain. This is proving to be a more acceptable way forward for some who, while remaining opposed to euthanasia, believe that the manner of the 'ending of life' is becoming a very difficult issue in our increasingly long-lived society.

The Christian conviction is that 'the life of men and women bears the stamp of God who "made man in his own image" (Genesis 1:27). This is the source of our basic dignity and it is the biblical basis for the sanctity of human life.' What God has given, we should not take away. Death is an event marking a transition rather than a terminus. We are called to use all God's gifts responsibly and to find in every situation the way of compassion. This compassion can be shown in energetically developing better methods of care for the dying. The hospice movement has made an invaluable contribution here.

Basis: Methodist Conference Statement on Euthanasia, 1974; *Shadows – A Study Pack on Euthanasia*, 1994, Methodist Church / Baptist Union.

The Russian Orthodox Church

Euthanasia

The Orthodox Church has always taught that euthanasia, which constitutes the deliberate taking of human life, is to be considered as murder. Yet advances in medical technology and new means of maintaining (and shortening) life have created a need for the clarification of this position.

The church, out of its position of compassion and concern, commends the use of measures which contribute to the comfort, relief of pain and overall well-being of a sufferer even when the use of such measures may have an undefined effect on the length of a patient's life. It also parts company with those who seek to prolong life at whatever the spiritual, psychological and material cost. Father Stanley Harakas writes:

> The Church, therefore, distinguishes between euthanasia and the withholding of extraordinary means of prolonging a life unable to sustain itself. It affirms the sanctity of human life and man's God-given responsibility to preserve life. But it rejects an attitude which disregards the inevitability of death. The only 'good death' for an Orthodox Christian is the peaceful acceptance of the end of his or her earthly life with faith and trust in God and the promise of the resurrection.

The right to die

The advances of modern technology provide artificial organs (kidney machines and so on) and life support machines which can be switched off, allowing a person to die. The Orthodox tradition does not provide us with specific guide lines for these developments. There are, however, several basic ethical traditions for our guidance.

God is the author of life and we have the responsibility to defend, protect and enhance life as a basis of living God's will. God is the giver of life, and 'in his hand is the life of every living thing and the breath of all mankind' (Job 12:10). To wrongfully take the life of an innocent person is murder and is condemned as sin (Exodus 20:13). On the other hand, 'it is appointed for men to die once' (Hebrews 9:27). Physical death is inevitable, yet it is something that comes normally despite our efforts to preserve life. There is something barbaric which calls for the 'elimination' of human life. Hence, the Orthodox Church completely and unalterably opposes euthanasia and yet does not support modern medical techniques which are so able to preserve life which God is struggling to take! Hence, when ordinary medical efforts are incapable of sustaining life, and when the body literally struggles to die, the Church prays as follows:

> Thou hast commanded the dissolution of the indescribable bond of soul and body, O God of spirits, and hast ordered them to be separated by Thy divine will. The body is thus to be returned to the elements from which it was made, and the soul is to proceed to the source of its existence until the resurrection of all. For this reason we implore Thee, the eternal and immortal Father, the Only-begotten Son and the All-Holy Spirit, that Thou bring about the peaceful separation of the soul of Thy servant (name) from his [her] body.

Hence, there are times when the Church prays that life might come to an end. Clear Orthodox Christian guidelines are thus available to us:

- we have the responsibility, as a trust from God, to maintain, preserve and protect our own lives and those lives entrusted to us;

- in case of illness, we are obliged to use every method available to us to restore health, both spiritual and medical;

- life is so precious and to be so respected that even when health cannot fully be restored, it should be protected and maintained;

- when, however, the major physical systems have broken down, and there does not seem to be any reasonable expectation that they can be restored,

Orthodox Christians may properly allow extraordinary medical devices to be removed.

The decision should never be taken alone. It should be shared by the family, if possible, and made on the basis of expert medical opinion. It should also be made with the advice, counsel and prayer of the priest.

This action should never be confused with euthanasia, which brings to an end, deliberately and consciously, a life which is capable of maintaining itself with normal care. It is one thing to kill and murder; it is quite another to 'allow the peaceful separation of soul and body'.

The Religious Society of Friends (Quakers)

Euthanasia

Friends are not united on the subject of euthanasia. (Please see the comments on how Friends develop testimonies in the section on Abortion) We would make a distinction between allowing someone to die whose life was being prolonged by medication or life support systems and so-called 'mercy killing' or euthanasia where a patient requests that a doctor administers an overdose or drug intended to cause death. There are some Friends who believe that people suffering, for example, great pain should be allowed to die with dignity and would wish the option of euthanasia to be available. Other Friends would say that if we care for each other and offer proper support, euthanasia should not be needed. Some Friends work in the Hospice movement which seeks to give patients proper pain relief so that the quality of life is maintained as death approaches.

The Advices say:

> Are you able to contemplate your death and the
> death of those close to you? . . . Accepting the fact of
> death, we are freed to live more fully.

In the light of this, some Friends may hold 'clearness meetings' to prepare themselves when they know that their death is likely, so that, with a small group of Friends in an atmosphere of worship, the issue can be faced openly and with love. On a related but slightly different question, some draw up 'living wills' requesting that they should not be kept alive at all costs should they ever reach a point where

they cannot make their wishes known. All Quakers are requested in Advices and Queries to draw up a will in order that their affairs should be in order at their death, out of consideration of those who are left behind.

Suicide

In the past Friends would bury suicide victims when the Established Church would not. Today they would hope that they can give individuals a feeling of love and support, so that a desperate solution becomes unnecessary. Many Friends are members of the Samaritans and work actively to help people who are despairing.

Organ donation

Many Quakers carry donor cards and some have received a transplant. On the other hand, some Quakers choose not to carry cards. It is a matter for individual choice.

The Roman Catholic Church

The foundation of catholic teaching on euthanasia is that human life is sacred and to be protected – only God is the Lord of life and death. Our time on earth is a pilgrimage of faith – it is not for a person themselves, or anyone else, with or without consent, to interrupt this journey before God calls him or her from this world to the life after death. The church is totally opposed to any action (for example, overdose, lethal injection – which would constitute murder) or the omission of treatment if the intention is to cause death at the patient's request (assisted suicide).

The Roman Catholic Church does not, however, argue that life must be preserved at all cost. Indeed, it would stress that we need to accept the reality of death and to prepare ourselves for it. A distinction is drawn between allowing death to occur when further treatment is futile or burdensome, and directly causing a person's death by act or omission. Treatment is commonly described as ordinary (proportionate) and extraordinary (disproportionate). Any treatment assessed to be extraordinary (futile, dangerous, or burdensome to patient, family or ultimately society) need not be accepted.

The Catechism of the Catholic Church states that:

> The decisions should be made by the patient if he is competent and able, or, if not, by those legally entitled to act for the patient, whose reasonable will and legitimate interests must always be respected (CCC §2278).

The use of advance directives, or 'living wills', is problematic. There is no doubt that some forms encourage euthanasia. A carefully-worded statement of wishes in line with catholic teaching can, however, be of great benefit and ethically acceptable. One particularly difficult question, which often arises with advance directives, is that of whether the giving of food and water by drips to patients in comas or in a persistent vegetative state counts as ordinary care or extraordinary treatment. Opinions differ amongst both the medical profession and moral theologians because of the difficulties in diagnosing accurately states of unconsciousness (and distinguishing between them) and the potential for recovery in each case. A prudent approach maintains that food and water, being ordinary medical care, should continue to be administered.

A number of other difficult situations can be mentioned. The use of painkillers, such as morphine, which hasten death is acceptable because the primary effect and the intention is to relieve pain, not to cause death (CCC §2279). It is also acceptable to turn off life-support machines if continuation is medically futile. It is for the medical profession to determine when death has occurred.

Doctors, nurses and all healthcare workers in hospitals or hospices whose compassion and skills help those who are sick are also at the service of Jesus himself who said, 'As you did it to one of the least of these my brethren, you did it to me' (Matthew 25:40). They are called to build a 'civilisation of life and love' by humanising medicine – not contribute to the development of the euthanasian 'culture of death' as John Paul II calls it in Evangelium Vitae (1995).

The Salvation Army

The term 'euthanasia' describes any action taken with the primary purpose of deliberately accelerating the death of a patient, whether or not at the patient's request, in order to relieve distress.

Advocates of euthanasia insist that under certain conditions, any competent person should be permitted to 'choose to die'. They are anxious to avoid dying in conditions of pain, dementia or loneliness, or with loss of dignity, and fear the use of inappropriate life-sustaining measures made possible by modern technology.

Whilst recognising such anxieties, The Salvation Army believes that people do not have the right to death by their own decision, whether procured by their own act or by the commissioning of another. Only God is sovereign over life and death.

The Christian sees death as the transition from earthly life to life eternal, and it is the experience of Christians that the grace of God can sustain through any ordeal or adversity. However, it is our conviction that anyone in need should be offered compassionate, comprehensive and effective care to the end. In so doing, dignity and self-worth are maintained for the patient and positive feelings are encouraged in those who will be bereaved.

In spite of safeguards, euthanasia can be associated with gross abuses; and distrust is fostered within families and between patients and their doctors. For many reasons coercion occurs and patients feel guilty if they do not comply. The 'right to die' becomes a 'duty to die'.

We share anxiety that people have concerning inadequate care, unrelieved suffering and inappropriate treatments, but maintain that these can be overcome without resort to euthanasia. The hospice movement has shown that pain can be eliminated or considerably eased in all cases with the proper administration of drugs and other treatments. Sophisticated palliative skills are also available.

For these reasons, The Salvation Army opposes any proposal to legalise euthanasia.

We urge that resources be invested to meet the mental, physical and spiritual needs of all patients and their loved ones. Research into pain control and other aspects of palliative care for the chronically and terminally ill is paramount. The provision of skilled nursing is an essential part of the management of serious illness. Development of home-care facilities and the hospice programme is a requirement for providing the necessary support for patients in need, and would allay present fears.

These resources should be available to every person according to his or her medical condition.

We acknowledge that:

• to withdraw futile or over-burdensome treatment whilst continuing to provide full palliative care constitutes good medical practice and is not euthanasia.

• when irreversible brain death has occurred, the withdrawal of life-support systems may be appropriate.

• a patient may refuse recommended treatment – it is not euthanasia if this refusal hastens death.

• it is not euthanasia if measures taken with the sole purpose of relieving pain or suffering coincidentally hasten death.

Positional Statement 6, revised January 1995.

There is no contribution to this section from the United Reformed Church

Section 7 • Prejudice and Discrimination

The Baptist Union of Great Britain

Baptist principle is egalitarian. Each and every person is loved by God and is equal before God. Baptists believe that this should be reflected in the life of the church and the life of our nation and, as a result, are opposed to discrimination on the grounds of race, sex, social class, accent, age, disability, marital status and so on. With this in mind, the Baptist Union has adopted an equal opportunities policy for its staff recruitment.

However, well-meaning statements and declarations, although they are often necessary, are insufficient. A great deal of prejudice is unconscious and requires continuous effort to redress it. This means that many Baptists support any positive efforts that are made in favour of women and of minorities, programmes that raise awareness of our own prejudices and projects which bring together people from different backgrounds, for example black and white Christians, so that we can listen to one another.

The kingdom of God knows no prejudice and no discrimination. In fact, it might be better to say that it discriminates in favour of the poor, the weak and the marginalised. The Church therefore has a particular responsibility to listen to these groups, to work with them and to support their attempts to improve their own conditions. Baptist principles suggest that we should be working to ensure that what is true of God's kingdom becomes true of the churches and of the nation. It is to our shame that it is not yet so.

The Church of England

The Church of England's concern with racial justice stems from a conviction that Christians must challenge racism if their claim to preach the Gospel is to be credible. The Church's teaching is clear: everybody is made in God's image and is of equal worth. The General Synod recognises that society comprises different racial, cultural and religious groups and that the Church has a duty to use the opportunity this offers for the enrichment of national and personal life. It sees its responsibility in standing firm against the false teaching of all movements that advocate racial hatred and division. It defines racism as the theory, prejudice and practice of disadvantaging or advantaging someone solely on the grounds of their colour, culture and ethnic origin.

Through debates in General Synod and the work of the Board for Social Responsibility, its Community and Urban Affairs Committee and the Committee for Minority Ethnic Anglican concerns, the Church continues to speak out against racism and for racial justice. These bodies are concerned both with racial relations and with representation of ethnic groups in church congregations, in the community, throughout the country and within the structure of the Church itself.

There is recognition that there is much to be done in all these areas and the Church was prepared to begin by looking at itself. The 1990 report *Seeds of Hope* identified that the structures of the Church itself were racist in the way that they operated. A second report, *The Passing Winter*, identified changes that were being and should be made in the Church as an institution.

Current concerns focus on the effects of British asylum, immigration and nationality law. The General Synod has called for a humane and non-discriminatory law, which enjoys the confidence of all communities.

The Church of Scotland

Equal opportunities and racism

The Church of Scotland is an equal opportunities employer committed to the principle of equality of opportunity for all its employees and members without reference to gender, race, social position, political belief, age or disability. This policy aims to ensure that no one is discriminated against because of ethnic and cultural differences. Racism is a violation of human rights which cannot be tolerated. The eradication of racism and other human rights violations comes through changing attitudes by changing institutional power structures. The Church has a commission to stand with the oppressed and confront the oppressor.

Asylum and sanctuary

Like all other major European states, the United Kingdom now receives an increasing number of applications for asylum. More people are being driven from their countries because of ethnic and nationalist disturbance, conflict and war. The Bible tells Christians to be generous and welcoming, especially to people facing difficult situations – which obviously includes those who have to flee their own country.

Church of Scotland has called on HM Government to treat those seeking asylum in Britain much more generously, compassionately, efficiently and sensitively and has encouraged all in the Church to help asylum seekers suffering difficulties.

The Church believes that an open and caring society is fundamental to the gospel's picture of the Kingdom of God, and so it opposes practices and attitudes which exclude people. Most asylum seekers are in a state of shock, alarm, poverty, and ignorance of our language, procedures and culture, but given time, understanding and acceptance, they are likely to integrate into our society and play a valuable part in it. Britain, with its history of high emigration should be the first to admit the fairness of immigration opportunities.

Ecumenical Statement

The full Assembly of the Council of Churches for Britain and Ireland (now renamed Churches Together in Britain and Ireland) was in session when the MacPherson Report on the racist murder of Stephen Lawrence was published in February 1999. The Assembly responded to the report with the following statement.

> We, the members of the Council of Churches for Britain and Ireland Assembly at Swanwick, welcome the MacPherson Report on the Stephen Lawrence Enquiry addressing the need for radical change in the police service and other public institutions in Britain. We recognise the need to expose and deal with the institutional racism in our own churches and to strive together with other institutions to build a society free from hatred, violence and discrimination based on race, colour or creed. Racism is a pernicious, ingrained and insidious evil which cannot be tolerated. It is contrary to the Gospel of Jesus Christ. Racism kills. The God of Life we worship and celebrate calls us to work for the protection of life.
>
> The Report sets out lessons for us all and we must take a lead in valuing and celebrating the cultural diversity which now exists in these islands. We call for a careful

and serious response from the police, from our churches and from every sector of society. We commit ourselves to evaluate the report, its recommendations and their implications and to work for a society based on mutual respect and social justice.

> We look to the Churches Commission for Racial Justice to assist us in our continuing response to the Report as we seek to co-operate with others in forging a spirit of reconciliation and restoration in our countries
>
> Nothing can undo the terrible loss to the Lawrence family or their appalling experience during the past six years. We pay tribute to their courage, dignity and tenacity in pursuing justice and a better society, and we assure them of our solidarity and our prayers. A lasting memorial to Stephen must surely be a commitment to the eradication of racism wherever it exists.

The Methodist Church

Racism is prejudice plus power in defence of or to the advantage of one racial group or individual over against another less powerful one. 'Whatever our skin colour or background we are one in our common humanity and one in Christ.'

All are equal before God. Adverse discrimination on the basis of racial or cultural characteristics contradicts our common humanity and the Gospel. To judge anyone adversely solely on account of his or her membership of a class or a racial group is to violate his or her status as a human being. Intelligence, educational capacity, character and quality of personality are independent of racial characteristics.

Racism leads to resentment and violence. It is contrary to the interests of the community as a whole. Christians are called to work against racism by becoming aware of it and counteracting it in themselves, learning to recognise its organisational forms, and campaigning against it wherever it appears: in immigration and nationality law, in the criminal justice system, in housing administration, in provision of educational and training facilities, or in relations between police and ethnic minorities. A Methodist Conference Statement on Racism contains the following affirmations:

> We reaffirm that Racism is a direct contradiction of the Gospel of Jesus.

We welcome the multiracial nature of society in Britain and assert our unqualified commitment to it. We regard it as economically, socially, culturally and spiritually beneficial for total human development.

Basis: Methodist Conference Statement on Racial Justice, 1987.

The Religious Society of Friends (Quakers)

Racial discrimination

The beginnings of Quakerism coincided with the development of the Atlantic slave trade. Some Quakers owned slaves; others saw the evil of slavery. By 1676 George Fox was writing that Christ

... died for the tawnies and the blacks as well as for you that are called whites ... [and] hath enlightened them as well as he hath enlightened you; and his grace hath appeared unto them as well as it hath unto you.

From this fundamental idea of the Inward Light in every person, Fox reasoned that the servitude of negroes (as they were then called) should end, just as the law of Moses provided that bondsmen should be set free after a time. And, Fox added, 'when they go, and are made free, let them not go away empty-handed.'

Quakers grew in understanding of the evils of slavery, helped by two key figures, Benjamin Lay (1682–1759) and John Woolman (1720–72). By 1758, Philadelphia Yearly Meeting had decided to disown (exclude from membership) those who bought or sold slaves. By 1783, Meeting for Sufferings was petitioning Parliament to forbid the slave trade.

A passage in Woolman's journal exemplifies for Quakers the ideal of an equal relationship respecting that of God in the other. He was on a journey to visit some native Americans, or Indians, in an area where some had 'slain and scalped English people in divers places'. Rain kept him in his tent and ...

I was led to think on the nature of the exercise .. love was the first motion, and then a concern arose to spend some time with the Indians, that I might feel and understand their life, and the spirit they live in, if haply I might receive some instruction from them, or they be in any degree helped forward by my following the leadings of Truth among them.

In 1989 the Community Relations Committee of London Yearly Meeting wrote:

There is a unity which goes beyond the physical characteristics and deeper than personal endowment. We have found again and again that there is an inward spirit – that of God in every one. At the deepest level of all, members of the human race are one family.

Personal experience of individual Quakers both leads to and confirms their Testimonies on harmony and equality.

Nonetheless, being a Friend does not confer automatic protection against unthinking assumptions and insensitivity. So, in 1988, Meeting for Sufferings recorded a Statement of Intent on Racism reminding British Quakers that 'The Religious Society of Friends has a duty to play its part in ending these abuses. Being aware of injustice and doing little about it condones that injustice.' It would be safe to say that no Quaker is involved in a racist organisation and that, whatever their political party, trade union or other group, they try to work for harmony and against prejudice.

The newly set up Committee for Racial Equality will offer individuals and Meetings information and advice, helping Friends to have the honesty and courage to examine the roots of their own prejudice and fear, and then take action. This committee, with the Parliamentary Liaison Secretary, will also act at a national level, making representations to government on relevant bills. Within the Society, the Statement continues, 'we shall keep under review our corporate practices in employing staff, obtaining goods and services, making investments, and engaging with the wider society.'

Sex discrimination

Among Quakers, priesthood belongs to the gathered meeting, and the work of a priest is shared among the members. There are no ordained, separated priests or ministers. Both women and men play a full part according to their abilities and experience – as do young and old, able and disabled, new attenders and more seasoned members – whether speaking in Meeting for Worship or carrying out one of the many tasks necessary in any community. In the 17th century, the sense of equality was expressed through separate men's and women's business meetings with different functions, the latter having responsibility for all pastoral care, including marriages. By the mid-19th century, the need for such positive discrimination had faded, and all business meetings were united. Quakers are nonetheless influenced by the society in which they live, so that work is still needed to reach actual equality. There is a need to look for more women Treasurers and more men Overseers (responsible for pastoral care) for example. Sexist language also needs attention, and the Friends who approved *Quaker Faith and Practice* at the 1994 Yearly Meeting had this very much in mind.

The Roman Catholic Church

A recent statement of the Church's teaching, *The Church and Racism*, was published in 1989, but as early as 1537 Pope Paul III denounced those who held that 'the inhabitants of the West Indies and the southern continents ... should be treated like irrational animals and used exclusively for our profit'. In 1888, Pope Leo XIII denounced the slave trade in his encyclical *In Plurimis* and the report recently published was issued to coincide with the centenary of Leo XIII's charter.

The present document summarises the historical picture, and focuses on forms of racism today. It sees racism in 'troubling new manifestations' that can be seen 'in various forms'. The obvious institutionalised racism of South Africa is one such, but consideration is also given to the position of aboriginal peoples, religious minorities of different ethnic groups, refugees and immigrants, as well as those affected by social and spontaneous racism and anti-Semitism.

The teachings of the Second Vatican Council, taken with those of Paul VI and John Paul II, have strongly reinforced the Church's teaching against racism. Three basic concepts have to be taken note of, namely:

1 Recognition of diversity and complementarity should lead to respect for differences.

2 Charity and justice should be so directed that everyone should be able to have dignified living conditions which should lead to a development of fraternity.

3 This in turn should lead to effective solidarity between all races.

The document continues to suggest how Catholics, working together with other Christians and indeed all who have a deep respect for persons, can promote fraternity and solidarity. It sees the role of schools as vital, in their teaching as well as in examining the ways in which they may be responsible for racist attitudes. The Church calls for action, for support of present programmes and for initiatives, and sees her mission to 'give soul to this immense undertaking of human fraternity ... every person is my brother or sister'.

The Salvation Army

The Salvation Army, as a branch of the Church, opposes discriminatory practices related to race or national origin at all levels of operation and administration, and seeks to promote inter-group understanding and to give full support to the imperatives of human and civil rights, not only at the levels of housing and education and employment, but also in the areas of culture and religion, sharing that spiritual affinity which makes all men brothers. More specifically:

1 All Salvation Army positions to which officers or employees are normally appointed are open to persons of any race who have the necessary qualifications or skills.

2 All social welfare services to individuals or families are given without regard to race.

3 All Salvation Army worship services are open to persons of any race, and spiritual ministrations are made available to all.

The Salvation Army from its inception has been concerned with the spiritual and social needs of all people. Its services in all parts of the world have been developed in recognition of the biblical principle that God 'has made from one blood every nation of men to dwell on all the face of the earth' (Acts 17:26).

Positional Statement 9, reissued November 1992.

The United Reformed Church

The Church's attitude to prejudice and discrimination is founded on the biblical concepts of creation and redemption.

1 Creation

All human beings are made in the image of God (Genesis 1:26) as the summit of God's creation. Human beings are made for each other, to live in community and to have corporate responsibility for the whole of creation (Genesis 2:19–20). But unlike the rest of creation there are no separate species within humanity. There is only one human race. What we call 'races' are nothing more significant than slight variations of the basic human stock (Acts 17:26 and Genesis 3:20).

2 Redemption

In Jesus Christ the barriers between humankind and God are broken down. Similarly the divisions within the human family are destroyed (Ephesians 2:13–18). Reconciliation with God is to become part of a new humanity in which all human distinctions of race, class, sex or status cease to be reasons for hostility and division (Galatians 3:28; Colossians 3:11; James 2:5–9). In Christ the unity of humankind is restored (Ephesians 2:19–22) – now it is based upon faith in God.

The following Declaration on Racism was debated and agreed at the General Assembly of the United Reformed Church in May 1987:

Creed
The United Reformed Church believes that all people are created in God's image, free and equal in his sight.

Definition
Racism results where prejudiced attitudes of superiority over others are combined with the power to shape society

History
Western civilisation is, and has long been, seriously flawed by racism.

Acknowledgement
British society nurtures racism through assumptions, stereotypes and organisational barriers which deny black people a just share of power and decision-making.

Confession
The church displays racism by failing to adapt so that black people can share fully in its life, its outreach and its decision-making.

Affirmation
There is cause for celebration in church and society when black and white people learn to co-operate, share power and make decisions together and where new forms of community life are thus discovered.

Commitment
The United Reformed Church commits itself to challenge and equip all its people to resist racism within themselves, within the church and within society as a whole and to train people and devote resources to this task.

Pledge
The United Reformed Church pledges itself, as it shares in action against racism, to monitor and review at regular intervals what progress is being made in church and society.

Section 8 • Law and Order

The Baptist Union of Great Britain

Baptists believe that the State has a role, under God, to enable its citizens to live free, peaceful and productive lives. the State is therefore responsible for the maintenance of the just order that is required for this to be possible. The law is one of the means by which the State may maintain just order. Where necessary, the State must punish those whose actions disturb the just order of society and so interfere with the freedom, peace or productivity of others

Since the State is instituted by God, Baptists are normally obedient even when they regard certain laws as wrong. The key issue for them is whether the State is fulfilling its true function; if it becomes oppressive and interferes with freedom, especially religious freedom, then many Baptists would be prepared to resist the State in the hope of bringing about change.

Baptists in Britain and elsewhere have always been a religious minority and in less tolerant ages and countries they have been persecuted and regarded as second class citizens because of their faith. For this reason Baptists have always spoken out in favour of religious liberty and have defended their own rights and the rights of others to freedom of conscience.

Punishment

The purpose of punishment is a debated issue in our culture. Some believe its purpose is retribution, some that it should be used as a deterrent while others believe that its purpose is to reform the criminal. It may be that different purposes are appropriate in different cases.

What is certain is that victims of crime and those close to them are often prepared to take the law into their own hands if they regard a criminal as unpunished or insufficiently punished. Such actions would soon lead to social chaos. Punishing criminals is therefore one of the means by which the State maintains order.

In Britain today most punishment is done by means of fines and prison sentences. Many Baptists have started to question whether imprisonment is an effective form of response to crime. Some evidence suggests that it does not always produce the effects desired. There is a strong case to be made for researching alternative ways of responding to crime, such as requiring criminals to do community service and requiring them to make reparation to their victims. More recognition should be given to the trauma caused to victims and more adequate victim support schemes may be needed.

There are many Baptists who believe that while all humans are responsible for their own actions, social conditions do affect crime levels. Governments therefore have a responsibility to address these issues as well as those of punishment when they formulate their public order policies.

Capital punishment

Capital punishment is certainly effective at persuading victims of crime not to take the law into their own hands. It may therefore be considered as useful in promoting public order. However, many Baptists are opposed to it. Firstly, human systems of justice are fallible and so innocent people might be executed. Secondly, the possibility of repentance and of the restoration of right relationships is permanently lost.

The Church of England

This section covers many issues in relation to how society is organised and how law and order is maintained, to enable people to live peacefully and in freedom. The biblical and theological principles underlying the Church of England's statements on these issues relate to a commitment to justice and mercy, the reality of sin and the need for repentance, forgiveness and reform, and most importantly, the worth of every individual as created in the image of God. The Church encourages ongoing study of these principles, which lie at the root of any penal system commended by the Church.

A criminal justice system must not only be merciful, but should also exhibit that exercise of mercy against a background of fundamental justice in which a delicate balance is maintained against competing self-interests and rival moral claims.

General Synod debates focus on particular concerns as they are raised within society. Recent debates have covered unsafe convictions, conditions in prisons and racial discrimination within the criminal justice system. The Church is concerned that there should be greater use of non-custodial sentences, that the prison population is too large, that conditions are often poor and that there is a need to improve remedial facilities in prison. It supports amendments to the Criminal Justice Bill that would prohibit by statute racial discrimination within the criminal justice system and an investigation of the reasons for the disproportionately large number of black people in prison.

The Board for Social Responsibility has a Home Affairs Committee which has recently produced a number of publications that focus on private sector involvement in prisons, young people and crime and the vulnerability of those in prison. The Board has made a number of practical suggestions in relation to various issues, for example, policing, crime prevention and detection, prosecution, forensic evidence.

The Church commends and supports those Christians who work within the criminal justice system and the Prison Chaplaincy Service.

In relation to capital punishment, the General Synod has stated that its reintroduction into the United Kingdom sentencing policy would be 'deplored'.

The Church of Scotland

God, being righteous, requires the recognition of wrongdoing. He is also a God of mercy and love identifying himself, through Christ, with humanity. The New Testament points out that we have all broken God's law and therefore stand under the judgement and grace of God. We therefore require the reconciliation and restoration offered by Christ.

The Church believes that the criminal justice system should reflect this relationship between God and his people. It should seek to restore the broken relationships between the offender and the community and discourage law breaking by punishment that is neither violent nor brutalising and that does not deny human dignity to anyone. It should also effect reconciliation

between the offender and his victim and society at large and should incorporate forgiveness.

The causes of crime are complex, stemming from poverty, unemployment, homelessness, drugs and a series of factors that are personal to the wrongdoer.

It is important that Christians are informed on these issues and seek to respond to the problems of crime in a way that reflects this complexity. The long term prevention of crime requires action on poverty and programmes to promote social inclusion.

The action to be taken with offenders must have a creative purpose. Sentencing needs to inform the offender that they have done wrong. It needs to give guidance on how they should change, give them the opportunity to change and reinforce their sense of personal responsibility.

The victims of crime need support and care both through the existing support schemes and by the pastoral work of prison chaplains, congregations and ministers. Victims are often frustrated by the lack of information and support given to them during the prosecution of the offender and this is an issue that needs to be addressed.

The church has a pastoral concern for the police and prison officers and all those who administer the criminal justice system.

The Methodist Church

Law and order

God brought the world into existence not for chaos but for order. In the sphere of human behaviour, order is preserved by customs and laws dealing with such matters as the enforceability of contracts, unjustified violence, and the protection of property.

The law must constantly be checked and updated for fairness. Respect for justice may require that particular laws are vigorously contested and reformed. Where a law, or a particular government, is gravely unjust, and incapable of reform through the political process, Christians may be called to non-violent civil disobedience in protest. This will be rare in the relatively just, relatively open, relatively democratic society in which we live, where there are many opportunities to draw attention to unjust laws and where argument and campaigning can bring about reform.

Basis: *Accept and Resist*, Methodist Conference Report, 1986.

Punishment

Christians recognise that Government has a duty on behalf of society to protect that society from crime for the common good. Those found guilty of breaches of the law may be punished. The punishment will include an element of retribution, but the aim of punishment is not primarily retribution, still less revenge, but the reform and rehabilitation of the offender. Greater emphasis should be placed on community-based resources, particularly in respect of young people who break the law.

Basis: *Breaking Out: A Christian Critique of Criminal Justice*, Adrian Speller, Collins, 1987; *Criminal Justice*, Methodist Conference, 1994.

The Religious Society of Friends (Quakers)

A central accepted belief of Friends is that there is 'something of God' in all people, and that each human being is of unique worth. This shared belief has led Quakers to attempt to value all people and not to harm or threaten them. What this means in their daily lives, is that most Quakers feel that everyone should be respected and treated decently, even if they have committed a crime.

The issues of crime and punishment are of great importance to the Society of Friends, and they have a history of links with the punishment system both here in Britain and in the United States of America.

The Religious Society of Friends, or Quakers, emerged in the troubled mid-1600s in Britain. The problems in the society of the time led George Fox and others to seek for what they felt was the Truth. Friends did not participate in what was then the religion of the State, and they were often regarded as criminals as a result. George Fox spent nearly six years of his life in prison, and by 1689 1,500 Friends had been in prison and 450 had died there due to the terrible conditions.

When seeking guidance on such issues as crime and punishment, Quakers look to writings such as those gathered together in *Quaker Faith and Practice*. For example:

The terrible sufferings of our forefathers in the prisons of the seventeenth century have given us as people a special interest in the management of prisons and the treatment of crime. George Fox protested to the judges of his day 'concerning their putting men to death for cattle and money and small matters', and laid before them 'what hurtful thing it was that prisoners should lie so long in jail', showing how 'they learned wickedness from one another in talking of their bad deeds'.

Elizabeth Fry (1780–1845) regularly visited Newgate prison to attend to the needs of the women and children there who were forced to live in terrible conditions. She campaigned against transporting prisoners to Australia, against capital punishment and for reform in prisons.

Quakers have always had strong views on capital punishment. In 1818 the following statement was made:

The awful subject of the punishment of death at this time deeply impressed our minds. We believe that where the precepts and spirit of our great Lord and Lawgiver have a complete ascendancy, they will lead to the abolition of this practice.

John Bright, the first Quaker member of Parliament, said in 1868:

The real security for human life is to be found in a reverence for it … A deep reverence for human life is worth more than a thousand executions in the prevention of murder; and is, in fact, the great security for human life. The law of capital punishment while pretending to support this reverence, does in fact tend to destroy it.

Today, Quakers are deeply concerned for those who are involved with crime and are 'punished' by our present system. Quakers are aware that Britain punishes more people by imprisonment than any other country in Europe. Most Friends accept that some criminals are so dangerous that they need to be confined, but these are a very small minority of those in prison. Experience in prison can badly damage people, and it rarely stops crime. Prison is punishment not only for offenders but also for their families. Most Quakers feel that other forms of sentencing such as community service are far preferable, and should be used more. Some Friends are appointed Prison Visitors or Prison Chaplains; others work towards the ideal of a non-punitive society. Many are actively supporting restorative justice and look forward to a wider acceptance of such positive approaches.

In 1998, the Quakers' Crime and Community Justice Committee issued a discussion paper. The following is an extract:

> As Friends, our approach to crime and criminal justice is a reflection of our deeply held belief in the value of each human being as a unique, precious child of God. This includes the victims of crime, the offenders, and those other members of society, less directly affected. Each of us has the ability to grow and change, to make amends, to learn what is right and what is wrong and to make a positive and valuable contribution to society. Friends also believe that the Kingdom of God is achieved through justice and peace for all of God's children. In the words of *Mending the Harm: Friends and Restorative Justice*: 'Retributive justice dictates revenge, not healing, and demands punitive sanctions instead of addressing the needs of the victim, the offender and the community.' Such an approach is unlikely to help bring about the Kingdom of God. Our response to crime must therefore be fair to all those affected: victims, offenders, and the community, and – most importantly – it must leave room for reconciliation and restoration of positive relationships within the community.

> Crime and criminality do not exist in isolation. We know that there are a range of social issues which are interconnected and we therefore appreciate that the solutions must also be found in a context which is wider than the criminal justice system alone. Most influences on criminality and social breakdown lie elsewhere and should be tackled where they are found. The purposes of the criminal justice services should not be seen narrowly as controlling and punishing crime, but as public services in a broader sense – protecting the weak and vulnerable and promoting social stability and public safety.

The Roman Catholic Church

Punishment

There are three purposes commonly accepted for punishment:

1 **Retribution**. The person is made to suffer for doing something wrong.

2 **Remedial**. The criminal will change his or her ways.

3 **Deterrence**. Others will be deterred from misbehaving.

These reasons for punishing give rise to complex issues in the philosophy of justice and political philosophy. What are the reasons for particular punishments for particular crimes?

By depriving criminals of some good, punishment makes it plain that they are not entitled to share in the benefits of life in an orderly society, for they have attacked the order of society. Punishment denounces the crime, and ensures that the criminal does not enjoy the fruits which belong, by right, to good behaviour.

Where, however, would capital punishment fit into the categories being discussed?

Rarely does any Christian theologian want to argue that retribution is the moral justification for any form of punishment. Usually arguments are based on either the remedial or the deterrent value of punishment. Clearly the death penalty can only by used as a deterrent, and the arguments are not convincing.

Capital punishment

The Catholic Church has never officially condemned the death penalty. However a number of authoritative voices in the Church have called in recent years for its abolition. These include: the Canadian Bishops; the Justice and Peace Commission of the Irish Bishops, 1976; the Justice and Peace Commission of the United States Bishops, 1977; the Social Commission of the French Bishops, 1978; the Bishops Conference of the United States, 1978.

The history of Christian thinking on the subject suggests that the theological arguments are not conclusive in either direction, for or against the death penalty.

Among the early Fathers of the Church, both views can be found, but the right of the State to execute criminals was defended in extreme circumstances. The early Church did try to influence the legal code in the direction of mercy and correction, but did not succeed altogether. Thomas Aquinas taught that in this life punishment has two purposes, to secure the reform of the sinner and the peace of society. Punishments are not sought for their own sake. For Aquinas the good of society took precedence at times over the reform of the criminal, and in this case he saw the death penalty as permissible.

During the middle ages not only was the State's right to use the death penalty defended but the Church itself wanted to ensure that it was used in cases of heresy!

During the 19th century the movement against the death penalty gained a little momentum. However even during the first part of the twentieth century, while abolition is favoured, the death penalty is not absolutely condemned, as it is allowed that it might be necessary under exceptional circumstances.

There are several good reasons put forward by theologians for not restoring the death penalty.

1 First and foremost it undermines the respect for human life. Respect for life is like a seamless garment. When the State executes it is helping to diminish respect for human life.

2 Mistakes can be made in the judicial system. People can be released from prison when a mistake is uncovered but, if executed, no remedy is possible.

3 A disproportionate number of those executed come from among the poor and the underprivileged. It seems fairer to recognise that those subjected to the greatest pressures may not be as fully responsible for their actions as they seem to be, and refrain from using the most serious penalty against them.

The Salvation Army

Capital punishment

The Salvation Army recognises that the opinions of Salvationists are divided on the moral acceptability of capital punishment and its effectiveness as a deterrent.

However, to advocate in any way the continuance or restoration of capital punishment would be inconsis-

tent with the Army's purposes and contrary to its belief that all human life is sacred and that each human being, however wretched, can become a new person in Christ. Long experience in rendering service within the criminal justice systems of many lands, has confirmed the Army's belief in the possibility of forgiveness and redemption for all.

Arguments based on scripture are used both to support and oppose capital punishment, the former drawing primarily on the Old Testament and the latter on the New Testament. The Army recognises that those laws of the Old Testament have been superseded in Christ and that a literal adherence to them today would require the death penalty for relatively minor transgressions. Equally, the New Testament does not attempt to provide a systematic treatment of criminal justice, nor does it offer conclusive comment on how society should deal with crime and its perpetrators.

Salvationists seek to understand how the God they worship identified himself with sinners through the life of Jesus, who was unjustly executed as a criminal in degrading circumstances. It was and is the mission of Jesus to pay penalty of sin within and thereby to make possible the transformation of the character of the offender, who is precious in God's eyes and worthy of redemption.

The Salvation Army acknowledges the need of society to be protected from wrongdoers, especially those willing to use violence, but recognises also the responsibility placed upon society so to regulate itself that the dignity and worth of all persons are made paramount and that the lowest instincts of men and women are not incited or inflamed. Special responsibilities in this regard fall upon publishers, broadcasters, legislators and educators. There is equally a role for the Church, the judiciary, the medical profession, and penologists to co-operate in advising government on both crime prevention and the development of just and humane penal systems.

Positional Statement 3, revised January 1992.

The United Reformed Church

Capital punishment

The URC, like most of the churches in Britain, is opposed to capital punishment and has, through the

British Council of Churches, on several occasions supported approaches to Members of Parliament when this matter was being debated.

This view is based on the principle that human life is sacred and that we do not have the right even in the case of those who have committed dreadful crimes, including the murder of others, to take their lives as punishment. The URC believes that even the most depraved person is capable of reform and that it is society's role to offer that possibility of reform through the systems of confinement and imprison-ment which the State organises. That, of course, does not imply satisfaction with the present arrangements for prisoners. There is much need for a reform of the prison system so that it can offer a better environment within which reform and change can take place.

Another reason for not supporting the death penalty is the possibility of human error in reaching a verdict. This is not the main reason for being opposed to it but it is a practical reason which adds weight to the objection in principle.

There is no contribution to this section from the Russian Orthodox Church

Section 9 • Work

Because the Council of Churches for Britain and Ireland (now renamed Churches Together in Britain and Ireland) published a major report on *Unemployment and the Future of Work* in 1997, it was unanimously agreed among the Churches contributing to this book that we would only print the ecumenical statement in this section.

Ecumenical Statement

In 1995, the Council of Churches for Britain and Ireland (CCBI) launched an enquiry in response to growing concerns about unemployment and the future of work. The CCBI is the ecumenical body to which almost all the main churches of Britain and Ireland belong. The findings of the Enquiry were published in April 1997 in the report *Unemployment and the Future of Work*.

The how and why

Method

A working party was established to carry out the 18-month long enquiry. Members of the working party represented a wide variety of backgrounds, regions and churches. The working party visited all four nations of the United kingdom and Ireland, speaking to:

• people with personal experience of unemployment and poverty

• people in positions of power and influence

• those with technical expertise in economics and social policy

• those that are tackling the problem of unemployment in various practical ways

Broad aim

The aim of the Enquiry was to 'analyse the various emerging trends (in employment) and evaluate the policy options from a Christian standpoint'.

Rationale

The rationale for the Report is summarised in this statement from the Second Vatican Council:

> The joy and hope, the grief and anguish of the men of our time, especially of those who are poor and afflicted in any way, are the joy and hope, the grief and anguish of the followers of Christ as well.
> (*Gaudium et Spes*)

Underlying the social issues that the Report attempts to address are spiritual ones. Spiritual issues include the waste of the God-given talents of the unemployed, sharing their pain and rebuilding the communities which unemployment has destroyed.

The Report quotes the organiser of Tearfund as saying:

> When people at the bottom of society's heap are treated with dignity and respect, their spiritual needs start to be addressed.

Reaction

The Report was published at the height of the election campaign and provoked widespread publicity and debate. The most controversial of its conclusions was the call for the redistribution of resources through the taxation system. At a time when the Labour Party was pledging not to raise income tax if it came into power, the Report concluded that:

> When so many are living in poverty and unemployment, it is wrong to give priority to those who are already well off.

A theology of work

The framework for the Report is a vision of work based on the following principles:

• Work is an offering of life, service and creativity to God and community.

- All work, such as that carried out by carers and parents, is to be valued, not just economically productive work.

- Everyone has a vocation, a role to play; there is a duty, and a right, to work and earn in a way most appropriate to the gifts given by God.

- Exploitative employment contracts are unacceptable as they fail to recognise the value and dignity of every individual.

- Work needs to be part of the rhythm of a full life, with time for rest, reflection and relationships.

Labour market trends

Questions asked by the Enquiry include:

- Could we create enough jobs to go round?
- Will there be enough jobs for the next generation?
- Should everyone have a right to a job?
- Does everyone have a duty to work?
- Are all jobs worth doing?

These questions must be answered in the light of a changing global market. Three main changes are identified as underlying labour market changes:

- The technological revolution.

- The growing numbers of women and declining numbers of men in the labour market.

- An increasingly flexible or deregulated labour market.

Consequences

The effect of these changes has been a growing divide in income and opportunity between those at the top and those at the bottom of our society. Defining poverty as having an income of less than half of average male earnings, a third of the poor in Britain today live in households where someone is working.

Policy recommendations

The Report identifies the strategic choices that face society. It also considers what economic and social policy measures are needed to put the principles implied by Christian faith into practice. The main finding of the Report is that:

> It is necessary and possible to create enough good work for all.

The Report recognises that this will require sufficient political will and public consensus. The Report also emphasises that these jobs should not be created at any price – 'service should not be servitude'. Many of the new jobs being created are low-skilled, low-paid and insecure.

Job creation

The Report recommends a mixture of job creation in the public, private and voluntary sectors.

One recommendation is that higher taxation should fund job creation in the areas of health care, education and community care.

Good employment

This requires decent and dignified conditions and pay. The Report highlights current problems such as overwork, grossly inadequate levels of pay and lack of quality, affordable childcare.

One recommendation was the introduction of a statutory Minimum Wage that should be set by a Low Pay Commission.

In April 1999, a National Minimum Wage was introduced in the UK. The level was set at £3.60 per hour with a lower rate of £3.00 for 18–21 year olds and £3.20 for those 22–24 year olds working on a New Deal employment option.

Lobby groups like Church Action on Poverty and many unions think that this rate is inadequate and are pushing for a rate of half median male earnings (£4.61 per hour).

Tackling unemployment

Priority needs to be given to tackling underlying labour market problems like skill mismatches. There may be many miners that are unemployed but they are unable to fill job vacancies in information technology.

Specific measures are also required to reverse long-term and youth unemployment.

The Report suggests the use of employment subsidies and public or voluntary work schemes.

The Government has introduced a series of 'new deals' for the unemployed. Among other things, these provide opportunities for some unemployed people to take up jobs that are subsidised for six months or to do voluntary environmental work.

Reform of the benefits system

Due to the interaction of employment and the benefits system, some people find themselves better off out of work than in work. For example, if someone moves from benefits into a job, they will have to start paying housing costs and Council Tax. If the job is low-paid, they may well have less money after paying these costs than if they had remained on benefits.

One recommendation of the Report is that benefits could be simplified by integrating in-work and out-of-work benefits.

Education and training

Provision for those with special educational needs is lower in the UK than other European countries and the proportions leaving school with no or few qualifications is higher. The less qualified find themselves disadvantaged in the labour market.

One recommendation is to create jobs in education and training to provide extra support for those with special educational needs.

Consulting unemployed people

Too often unemployed peoples' views and needs have been ignored and they have been widely portrayed as 'workshy'. The fact that many Government schemes for the unemployed have been, and still are, compulsory, is further reinforcement of the point. Within the New Deal for young people there is no option for 18–24 year olds that are unemployed to remain on benefits.

The Report emphasises that the vast majority of people that are unemployed would readily take up an offer of a good job if it were made to them.

The Report recommends that people that are unemployed should be consulted on matters concerning them and should have input in policy-making, perhaps in a newly established National Employment Forum.

Churches review use of resources

Although many churches and church members are involved in responding to unemployment in a variety of ways, the Report recommends that the churches reassess their use of resources in the light of need. Some churches could use their resources to create jobs that meet need in their local community or examine employment practices regarding their existing staff.

Putting principles into practice

Challenging greed

One current example of injustice evident in the area of employment is pay inequality.

Low pay is the single most important cause of poverty in the UK today. Currently, 20% of the population live in households receiving less than half of male median earnings. With the exception of New Zealand, the rate of increase in income inequality has been greater in the UK than in any other industrialised country.

According to research carried out in 1997 by The Guardian, the highest-paid directors now collect as much in a week as the average employee earns in a year. For example, in 1997, Sir Clive Thompson, chief executive of Rentokil Initial, earned £1.45 million while the average pay of his employees was £8,727. Sir Clive criticised calls for curbs on boardroom pay, such as those issued by the Chancellor, Gordon Brown, as 'undesirable'.

Challenging prejudice

The National Association for the Care and Resettlement of Offenders has consistently identified unemployment as a cause of crime, both before offending and after imprisonment.

It highlights the fact that 87% of prisoners face unemployment on release and encounter much prejudice when trying to find work.

According to a survey carried out by the Association of Chief Officers of Probation in 1997, only 7% of companies would actively consider a policy of recruiting trained ex-offenders (*Making A Fresh Start*, NACRO, 1998). Most employers are not willing to give ex-offenders a 'second chance' in the way we believe that God shows grace to us. This lack of faith compounds their problems. According to the Home Secretary, Jack Straw, 'A job is the best help that any ex-offender can get to avoid returning to crime.' (House of Commons, 30 July 1997)

There are no contributions to this section from individual churches.

Section 10 • Money Matters

The Baptist Union of Great Britain

Like Jesus, who is recorded as saying more about money than about heaven, Baptists believe that the way a believer treats money is an indicator of the seriousness of their discipleship. The opportunity to earn a living is a basic human right which affects a person's dignity, though compassionate provision must be made by state and voluntary agencies to safeguard those in society who find themselves in need. We are individuals who are precious to God, so no one's worth is to be measured by what they possess. Our possessions must not own us; they are to be used for our own benefit but also for the benefit of others, and above all for the glory of God. We are responsible to God not only for the amount we give to the Church or to charity but also for the way we use what we keep back for ourselves. This is a radical position, in a society that seemingly values a person by the amount of credit they can incur on a piece of plastic.

Baptists are generally against all forms of gambling and have come out strongly against the National Lottery, which is perceived as offering false values and hurting the poor. Baptist churches are strongly advised not to apply for Lottery funding, though local churches have the freedom to make their own choices (especially in situations where a partner in a project may be receiving Lottery money).

The Church of England

The Church of England is concerned on a personal level that individuals are wise with their money and live within their means and in a way which is aware of issues of inequality, stewardship and giving.

In recent debate, the General Synod has expressed its growing concern about the growth of personal debt and its implications particularly for poorer families. It called upon the members of the Church of England both locally and nationally in tackling this problem:

• by supporting representations to commercial, financial and official bodies whose activities are relevant to the problem;

• by contributing to efforts to reduce the adverse consequences of debt, for example by education in money management, debt counselling and protesting against pressure techniques;

• and by contributing their own Christian insights.

The Church of England is concerned on a political level that governments deal equitably and in a just manner in the financial management of society, always keeping in mind a concern for the most vulnerable. It advocates, for example, investment which is ethical and taxation which is fair.

In relation specifically to poverty, the Church of England recognises that many people, both old and young, are living on very low incomes and have real difficulty making ends meet. Often their health and family life suffer. The General Synod has reiterated the centrality of the poor in the concern of God and the implication of this for the life, work and witness of the Church of England. Christians are called to be among those working to reduce poverty.

The Church of Scotland

The Church of Scotland has criticised the Government for creating what it regards as a United Kingdom which is a gambler's paradise.

It is opposed to gambling in all its forms and so regards participation in the National Lottery as wrong. It has urged the Government to recognise that funds raised by this means are not an appropriate substitute for the responsible level of public funding, whether by voluntary contribution or taxation.

In its celebration of the year 2000 the Church has agreed not to make application to the Millennium Fund and not to make application to funds available through the National Lottery in order to support or develop its worship, witness, evangelism and pastoral care.

Debt is a soul-destroying experience for many people in a consumer society in which credit is persuasively advertised and credit cards are readily obtainable. However this should not distract us from the more widespread hardship that results either from a sudden drop in income (for example through redundancy or illness) or from chronic low income. The urgent need is to find ways of offering cheap and manageable credit to the poorest. Credit Unions where groups of people agree to save and lend together, may be part of the answer. A more realistic and effective benefit system would help.

The complicated way that benefits and the tax system work out means that some people find that they cannot afford to take jobs which are available to them. Others who work and are paid so little find themselves struggling to avoid debt. They are in work but living in poverty. The Church has supported a minimum national wage for all in employment as one way to tackles these problems and avoid the 'poverty trap'.

Ecumenical Statement

At the Churches Representatives Meeting held on 20–22 November 1995, the Council of Churches for Britain and Ireland (now renamed Churches Together in Britain and Ireland) accepted the statement of concern about the National Lottery prepared by a meeting of Social Responsibility Representatives the previous month.

1 We wish to affirm the public culture which has been of considerable benefit to our society. In this, money from taxation, charities working at national and local levels, central and local government have co-operated to sustain the common good.

2 We are deeply concerned that the National Lottery is undermining the public culture which has served us well. We therefore identify below some of our concerns about the way the National Lottery is adversely affecting our society.

3 We acknowledge, however, that lotteries are a pervasive feature of European life, and in many instances provide significant enhancement of public amenity.

4 All the Churches recognise that the National Lottery in the UK has provoked among their members a wide variety of opinion. In addition the National Lottery confronts the Churches with certain ethical dilemmas.

5 Our concerns about the National Lottery are the following:

5.1 One of the achievements of Government legislation in the 20th century has been the regulation of gambling. The National Lottery threatens recklessly to dismantle these regulations.

5.2 The National Lottery's huge advertising budget, coupled with publicity in the media, have created a considerable likelihood of gambling harm, with little prospect of public benefit.

The ready access to instant games, which are believed to be compulsive in character, illustrates the gambling harm.

The relatively small amount of money which will flow each year to charities from the Lottery is seen when it is compared with other sources of voluntary giving and public expenditure.

- Charity Board allocations: £1bn
- Total charitable giving: £10bn
- Social security expenditure: £70bn
- Total public expenditure: £300bn

5.3 Our widespread experience with charities and local government is that the overall effect of the Lottery is to reduce public expenditure rather than enhance public amenity.

5.4 The Lottery attracts expenditure from all sectors of society more or less evenly and therefore disproportionately from the poorest.

5.5 Our clear perception is that many vulnerable and desperate people are being induced to spend money on the lottery that they cannot afford.

6 We therefore call for authoritative and independent research on all aspects of the Lottery; in particular we wish Parliament urgently to revive the recommendation of the 1978 Royal Commission that a Gambling Research Council be established.

7 Until the research is available, we believe the Department of National Heritage and OFLOT should give serious consideration to the following

interim changes in the regulations of the National Lottery.

7.1 No more licenses for Instant Games to be issued.

7.2 The minimum age for playing the Lottery should be raised to 18 years.

7.3 The size of the jackpot prizes should be limited.

8 The most effective way of helping charities is by direct giving.

The Methodist Church

Jesus Christ taught his followers that they should use money in the right way (Luke 16). Methodists have for generations admired the advice of John Wesley on the use of money: earn all you can; save all you can; give all you can.

Earn all you can by diligence and persistence without harming yourself or your neighbour in body or soul. This means that you will not indulge in unfair practices such as undercutting prices or enticing away employees from a rival.

Save all you can by not spending money on unnecessary luxuries. Provide for the needs of your family and be content with a simple life.

Give all you can. God has created the whole universe. Everything we have is given to us in trust. We are stewards of our wealth to use it in a way acceptable to him. When the needs of your family are met, give to your fellow Christians and to the rest of mankind.

In recent years, market capitalism has been favoured in our society. Its principle is that buyers and sellers should be free to strike bargains without restraints on their activities. It has brought many benefits to a substantial part of the world's population. They have been able to fulfil themselves in many ways and gained pleasure from material possessions such as television. However there is immense cost when jobs are lost. The system causes pollution and uses up resources at a great rate. Astronomical salaries are paid to people in the City and grossly inadequate ones to people with other skills.

There is a movement to develop social responsibility in business. Good management practices include a high moral view of human relationships.

Self interest and competition are significant for success in business. Christians look for a community where gentleness and service are also highly prized.

The Methodist Church has continuing concerns about the National Lottery and its operation. First is the size of the prizes, particularly the rolled-over jackpots; second is the compulsive nature of the 'instant' lottery games such as scratch-cards; third is the minimum age for participation (16 years). On these issues, in partnership with ecumenical colleagues, the Methodist Church has made representations to the Government.

Basis: John Wesley, 'The Use of Money', Sermon 44; *Ethics of Wealth Creation*, 1991; National Lottery – Conference Decision, 1995. Other resources: *Statement on Gambling*, 1992; *Gambling and the Stock Exchange*, 1993; 'Through a Glass Darkly: some thoughts on the Ethics of Investment', Russell Sparkes Beckly Lecture, 1998.

The Religious Society of Friends (Quakers)

Principles

In *Quaker Views No. 6*, one of a series of pamphlets put together for pupils to help them understand Quaker approaches to various ethical questions, the author writes:

> If you believe that all people are the children of God, then Quakers would say that you cannot take advantage of others through any form of dishonesty, whether in buying or selling goods, in business or privately, or as employees by failing to give an honest return in labour for wages. When we receive goods or services we believe that bills should be paid promptly. 'The true function of business is not to rob the community, but to serve it.' Similarly, we do not try to evade the payment of taxes.

Here the use of money and conduct of business reflect the basic Quaker conviction of the need to answer 'that of God' in everyone. However financial issues are not relevant only for the individual. In 1987 the London Yearly Meeting (the former name for what is now Britain Yearly Meeting), troubled by an increasing inequality in British society, issued a statement on poverty in which it stated:

As a Religious Society and as individuals we commit ourselves to examine again how we use our personal and financial resources. We will press for change to enable wealth and power to be shared more evenly within our nation.

Life-style

Closely related to matters of economics and finance, are questions of life-style. Simplicity of living has been a Quaker testimony since the seventeenth century. Quakers are encouraged in their Advices and Queries:

> Try to live simply. A simple lifestyle freely chosen is a source of great strength. Do not be persuaded into buying what you do not need or cannot afford. Do you keep yourself informed about the effect your style of living is having on the global economy and environment?

National Lottery

These general principles give rise to the Quaker attitude to the National Lottery.

In December 1996, Meeting for Sufferings, the Standing Committee of Quakers in Britain, declared:

> The Religious Society of Friends (Quakers) in Britain has issued the following statement in response to two developments: the announcement of a second weekly draw and research findings about underage ticket sales:

> • The National Lottery offends our belief about loving neighbours and sharing resources. We wish to stand together, as members of the Council of Churches in Britain & Ireland (CCBI) and with all who share our values, against the rush to become a gambling society.

> • We consider our opposition to the promotion of the National Lottery to be part of our concern for truth and integrity in public affairs.

> • Therefore, we are totally opposed to the promotion of a large-scale lottery by Government and wish to see the National Lottery ended.

> • Meantime, we deplore the introduction of a National Lottery mid-week draw in addition to the existing Saturday draw.

> • We see the National Lottery as promoting the illusion of wealth as the ultimate fulfilment. It concerns us that obtaining wealth through chance and without effort is becoming an acceptable norm for British society.

> • We are disturbed by the accelerating substitution of National Lottery funds for planned public funding of important social projects.

> • We welcome the fact that the National Lottery Regulator, OFLOT, has undertaken and published its research findings on the incidence of under-age participation in the National Lottery, particularly the purchase of Scratchcards, and that more safeguards will be introduced by the licence-holder.

We strongly urge Parliament to take the further step of raising the age of legal sales from 16 to 18 years.

The Salvation Army

Gambling

Gambling is seeking gain at the expense of others, on the basis of chance.

The Salvation Army is acutely aware of the suffering and deprivation visited upon countless thousands of persons as the result of gambling. The Army's social welfare experience indicates that many of those who gamble frequently disregard their primary responsibilities in life and bring embarrassment and hurt to those dependent on them.

It also asserts that gambling is detrimental to the spiritual and moral well-being of those who participate without any apparent financial effects on themselves and their families.

Since all gambling is motivated by selfishness, it runs counter to the Christian expression of love, respect and concern for others. Often it begins in an apparently harmless way, but its continued practice tends to undermine the personality and character of the gambler and frequently leads to grosser excesses.

Official sanction and public acceptance of this evil is, in the opinion of The Salvation Army, contrary to the Christian principles to which it subscribes and it therefore opposes any extension of the provision of facilities for gambling, whether by government agencies, charitable organisations or commercial interests.

Salvationists are required to take no part in gambling in any form.

Positional Statement 7, 1992.

The United Reformed Church

General Assembly passed the following resolution in 1995.

National Lottery:
Assembly urges the members and councils of the church to disassociate themselves from the Lottery:
a) by refusing to buy tickets; and
b) by declining to apply for Lottery-generated funds for church purposes.

Church and Society has commented on this in each year since then, reporting on developments.

This particular paragraph was included in 1997 and unchallenged at Assembly. We therefore regard this as the *de facto* interpretation of the current situation.

Since the 1995 resolution, several local churches have become involved in applications for Lottery funding. Church and Society was asked by some to interpret the Assembly resolution. Our provisional response has been that, where the application is more broadly based than from a single church and where it seeks funding for projects to benefit the whole community and not merely or primarily the church and its organisations, this does not breach the spirit of what Assembly determined.

There are no contributions to this section from the Russian Orthodox Church or the Roman Catholic Church

Section 11 • Animal Welfare

The Church of England

The Church of England recognises that animals have been created by God and that they have an intrinsic value for that reason. Nevertheless, the value of animals has always been seen as secondary to that of human beings, who are made in God's image and placed in a central position in creation. Human beings have both an affinity with and an obligation to animals.

In dealing with animals, Christians need to recognise that they have a vested interest in controlling and regulating other species, and that this is part of the divine mandate for responsible stewardship. Biologically, humans are the most efficient predators of the animal world. For the Christian, this is a recognition that humans have dominion over all living things, and that this capacity needs to be regulated for our own and for other species' sakes. Careful husbandry towards all animals is both morally essential and sensible in practice.

The Church recognises the need for animals to be used in certain research to improve medical understanding, veterinary or behavioural knowledge, and to test for the safety of chemicals, and understands that such testing is a requirement of law. It also, however, affirms that responsible stewardship of the natural world requires all animals to receive careful and sympathetic treatment, both during their lives and in the manner of their dying.

In light of recent concerns related to the export of bull calves for veal production and the spread of Bovine Spongiform Encephalopathy (BSE or 'mad cow disease'), the General Synod urged for an improvement to the conditions in which livestock is transported. It also expressed support for British farmers and others adversely affected by the current confusion over BSE. These are cited as examples of how the Church of England is engaged in an ongoing and critical review of human responsibility to the living environment.

The Church of Scotland

The approach to animal welfare is based on the biblical doctrine of creation. Human beings are to be partners with God in caring for the environment and for all living things. Humane concern for animals is welcome provided it does not degenerate into sentimentality.

Farm animals

The main concern with intensive animal husbandry (factory farming) is the degree of freedom which the animals and birds are allowed. It is justifiable to assume that animals suffer in ways similar to human beings.

The Church believes that those involved must never allow economic considerations to be the sole deciding factor. Similarly the conditions under which animals are transported and loaded have to be monitored carefully. The journeys by road are often over-crowded, and sometimes fatal. A ban on the export of livestock for slaughter should be considered.

Animals used in experimentation

The competing claims of scientific research and animal welfare have to be kept in balance. While the use of living animals in experimentation for the purpose of saving or prolonging human life may be acceptable, undesirable trends must be controlled by legislation. For example some will question the use of animals for cloning experiments. Many have doubts about the necessity for animal experimentation in non-essential fields such as cosmetics. The purchase of cosmetics is an area where the public can exercise choice.

Animals in the wild

Hunting is not prohibited in the Bible. Where culling is necessary, for example seals and deer, the need to control numbers in the interests of conservation is recognised, but there is a need to ensure that unnecessary pain and suffering is not caused. In the same way while certain creatures may thrive in captivity in zoos and safari parks, there is a need to ensure that an appropriate environment is provided and it has to be recognised that this may not be possible for certain animals.

Performing animals

It is arguable that some animals may enjoy 'performing' in shows and circuses. It is also the case that it is wrong to keep large animals in the cramped conditions of cages. Caring inspection is necessary both of the living conditions of circus animals and of the methods used to train them.

Animals as pets

To avoid unnecessary cruelty and neglect of pets like dogs the Church has argued that a proper system of registration and tagging should be introduced.

The Methodist Church

The Bible records that God's covenant is not only with men and women, but 'with every living creature', and repeats it twice! A human being may be worth many sparrows, but even a sparrow does not die unnoticed (Matthew 10:29–31).

The Christian vision is of a world where the whole of nature is at harmony (Isaiah 11:6–8), and where none is exploited. Short of that ideal, as we are, the following judgements at least can be made.

Unnecessary and unjustifiable experiments and trials – as on the effects of cosmetics – should not take place. Intensive factory farming methods which ignore the welfare of animals are to be condemned. Every measure should be taken to preserve animal habitats.

Cruel sports, such as stag hunting and hare coursing, should be banned. The Christian attitude towards the animals who share creation with us should be one of responsibility and stewardship, not exploitation.

Basis: *The Treatment of Animals*, Methodist Conference Statement, 1980.

The Religious Society of Friends (Quakers)

Respect for animals is at the core of a Quaker understanding of reverence for life.

> Show a loving consideration for all creatures, and seek to maintain the beauty and variety of the world.
> *Advices and Queries* (1995)

In 1981 London Yearly Meeting (the forerunner of the present Britain Yearly Meeting) minuted:

> Our stewardship of the world does not allow us to exercise an absolute right over animals. All animals should be treated as if they have rights and as if they suffer pain and stress similar to human experience and differing only in degree. We have a duty to consider the consequences of our influence on the environment and its effects on animals, taking great care to reduce the harmful effects. Some activities, like killing for sport and aspects of trapping or hunting which involve cruelty in a slow death, are indefensible and we need to urge those who engage in these activities to reconsider their position.

In 1995, Meeting for Sufferings, the Standing Committee of Quakers, minuted:

> The discipline of the Religious Society of Friends (Quakers) in Britain asks us to 'show a loving consideration for all creatures,' and to 'work to ensure that our increasing power over nature is used responsibly with reverence for life.' We therefore are concerned for the welfare of animals.

> We ask the Government to take all possible steps to improve the treatment of animals used for food. We support the principle that slaughter of animals should take place as near to the farm where they have been reared as possible. Regulations, especially those regarding transport, should seek to reduce the risk of pain or suffering inflicted on animals. We urge the Government to work through European institutions to promote the highest standards of livestock welfare.

The Roman Catholic Church

Roman Catholic moral theology would deny that animals have rights. Its teaching focuses, rather, on human duties towards animals, especially with regard to the right use of them. To deny them rights is not to underestimate our obligations with regard to animal welfare. It is possible to oppose cruelty and exploitation without getting trapped in arguments about 'rights'. Discussion of animal welfare is placed within the context of our attitude towards creation as a whole. In recent years Church documents have become increasingly critical of the abuse of creation by our consumer society (see John Paul II, *Centesimus Annus*). Mistreatment of the natural world and of animals results from a faulty understanding on the part of humans: we forget that we too are part of creation and not its absolute masters. Created in the image and likeness of God (Genesis 1:26), men and women share in God's plans for the world. The account of creation in Genesis 1 shows men and women as stewards of creation. Our task is to make use of the world and its creatures but not to destroy, since creation is a good willed by God. We must hand it on to future generations. Our task is to protect and promote the good of creation; we do not have absolute dominion.

Animals, as our fellow creatures, should be a particular concern in our attitude towards creation. 'We owe them kindness.' (Catechism of the Catholic Church) The Roman Catholic Church teaches that certain uses of animals are acceptable: they can be used to provide 'food and clothing. They may be domesticated to help men and women in their work and leisure.' Official teaching tolerates their use in

medical and scientific experimentation 'if it remains within reasonable limits' and if this is contributing to 'caring for or saving human lives'. (All quotations from the *Catechism of the Catholic Church*)

That said, animals should not be caused 'to suffer or die needlessly'. One could use Roman Catholic teaching, therefore, to challenge irresponsible and unnecessary exploitation both for research and especially pleasure. The use of animals for food would also require consideration for potential suffering, both in slaughtering and in transport.

The Catechism warns also about exaggerated care being spent on animals, especially if money could be better spent on limiting human suffering. Catholic teaching, then, argues for a sense of balance. On the one hand animals are not the equals of human beings, they do not have human rights, but on the other as part of God's creation they are owed respect and appropriate care. The key concept is stewardship.

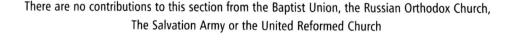

There are no contributions to this section from the Baptist Union, the Russian Orthodox Church, The Salvation Army or the United Reformed Church

Section 12 • Bioengineering

The Baptist Union of Great Britain

Advances in understanding of genetics and its link to disease raise a host of moral dilemmas. Baptists welcome greater scientific knowledge and the benefits for humanity, but are concerned about the impact of such technologies on the world, animals and human beings. All knowledge is to be exercised in responsibility to God, each other and to the created order of which we are stewards.

'The earth is the Lord's'. We are to exercise responsible dominion over the world. The destruction of species and of biodiversity by selective genetic engineering is reprehensible.

Animals are dependent on human beings. It is morally permissible to use animals for food and clothing, but that never justifies cruelty to animals, nor crossing genetic boundaries. The creation of hybrid animals or the genetic modification of animals, like pigs to produce organs for human transplantation, is to be carefully assessed not only for safety, but for what it does to animals as well as humans. Genetic modification of plants, flowers, vegetables and animals by selective breeding is well established. This is a way of feeding the hungry in the world, but also of producing great wealth. Concerns over genetically modified food focus on the loss of biodiversity, the environmental impact, crossing species boundaries, the risks from viruses and retroviruses and the development of super weeds and insects.

In relation to human beings, genetic testing, screening, therapy, manipulation and replacement raise moral concerns over our definition of what is normal, what is abnormal and what constitutes a handicap, fears of developing human clones in light of successful animal cloning, the selection of sex and of specific characteristics in children, and the control over reproduction ranging from sperm and egg selection to manipulation.

Baptists recognise that these possibilities affect our understanding of what it is to be human. Technology is God's gift, but may be abused. Human beings may be seen as nothing more than, and totally determined by, their genetic make up. Dehumanisation and depersonalisation easily follow. Bioengineering in fertility and genetics may relieve suffering, but raises concerns about the extent of interference, our sense of what is natural and fitting, and of how such information might be abused. Employment, insurance and mortgages will be transformed by the release of genetic information.

Society must be vigilant over the use of technology, create a clear moral framework for bioengineering and consider the effects on the world, plants and animals, human beings and society.

The Church of England

The Church of England is seeking to explore the whole area of bioengineering. Particular focus, at the present time, is on genetic engineering, in relation to plant and animal manipulation. Much media coverage has been given to these issues, from the 'creation' of Dolly the sheep, to genetically modified (GM) foods. The points raised below are intended to show something of the nature of this discussion.

At the centre of the discussion are theological and ethical issues relating to the belief that bioengineering is radically unnatural and to produce, for example, GM foods, is for human beings to be guilty of the hubris of 'playing God'. Certainly, they represent possibilities which could not come about without direct human intervention upon nature. Human beings are themselves part of nature, creatures within creation. Yet human discovery and invention can also be thought of as resulting from the exercise of God-given powers of mind and reason. Many have thought that the possession of these powers is part of what it means for humans to be 'in the image of God'.

It does not seem that radical 'unnaturalness' can of itself be the source of an ethical prohibition. It by no means follows, however, that everything that can be done should be done. There is a reverence due to the goodness of nature, seen as being God's creation. The Church wishes to offer wise counsel. This is unlikely to be either a recommendation for unrestricted exploitation or total prohibition, but for a careful consideration of individual proposals.

The Church of Scotland

Cloning animals

For the Christian, cloning seems to go against something basic and God-given about the variety in nature. The evolutionary need to maintain a basic level of genetic diversity reflects something of this. The church is not opposed to animal cloning where the main intention is not the clone itself, but to produce an animal of a known genetic composition where natural methods would not work.

What would be unacceptable would be to clone animals routinely for purely commercial reasons.

Cloning humans

The Church or Scotland agrees that to clone humans would be unethical and has called for an international treaty to ban cloning human beings world-wide. To make a genetic copy of an existing human being would violate the dignity and uniqueness of a person made in God's image. The notion of creating cloned embryos for research and then destroying them would be to treat a potential human being as disposable.

Genetic engineering modifying animals

For centuries, humans have been doing a type of genetic engineering by selectively breeding animals and plants to enhance particular genetic traits, like leaner meat or a higher growth rate. Now it is possible to manipulate specific genes in the laboratory, adding, deleting or altering genes to produce some desired effect. For the first time we can mix genes across very different species and this raises the question of what are, and are not, acceptable changes for humans to make in animals.

The Church believes that no serious ethical problems arise where genetic engineering of animals is used to produce proteins of medical value for the treatment of diseases such as emphysema and cystic fibrosis.

Serious questions are posed by genetically modified mice used as models for human genetic diseases or to test out possible therapies. The first example was the oncomouse, in which a human gene was added to cause the mouse to develop a mammary tumour. Medical researchers say they could make very little progress on treating such diseases without these mice. Animal welfare groups say that to force a mouse to get cancer in this way is a cruelly unacceptable use. There are two separate cultures, each driven by an overriding ethical criterion. There appears no simple answer. The inherent power in genetic changes means we should act with caution and humility, rather than indicating an absolute prohibition.

Animal organs for human transplants

Pigs' hearts might be used to overcome the shortfall in the 'supply' of human hearts, using genetic modification to trick the human body into thinking the heart was not from a foreign species. This 'xenotransplantation' is highly controversial. There may be a case for trying, but with a proviso about animal welfare. We should not be trying to make ourselves immortal by for ever changing worn out organs.

Genetically modified food

Some see genetic engineering opening up great opportunities in agriculture and food production. For others it is a threat to something very basic about ourselves and the natural world, unnecessary, harmful, unethical, and mostly benefiting big business at others' expense.

Claims are often made for the potential of genetically modified food to feed the world. For example, if genes could be manipulated to enable staple crops to grow in what are today marginal conditions, it could make a big difference to many countries which struggle to feed themselves.

However Christians are concerned that the driving forces of biotechnology are leading us to create unnecessary products for western indulgence, while the real food shortages elsewhere in the world remain neglected. The claim to feed the world will not be taken seriously until more biotechnological investment and expertise is focused on the needs of marginal agriculture in the Third World.

The Methodist Church

The Methodist Church has supported the scientific judgement that remedies for human infertility, and for certain genetic diseases and handicaps, would be greatly assisted if research on embryos not required for artificial insemination continues to be carried out. However, research should be restricted to the first fourteen days; in addition, embryos should not be brought into being specifically for research purposes.

It seems that through the 'engineering' or manipulation of the human genetic structure, there is a real hope of cure and relief for some very nasty and up till now incurable diseases and disabilities such as cystic fibrosis and muscular dystrophy.

Many questions arise. Is the human race right to pursue knowledge to discover more about our genetic make-up with all the possibilities for good and evil that might raise? Are human beings seeking to meddle in an area where they have no right to be? Would it be morally right to interfere with genes so as to 'improve' people, to make them more intelligent, or physically taller, or more 'handsome'? Some politicians and social scientists have wanted to do this in the past, but the Churches have condemned the science of 'eugenics', especially since the dreadful experiments conducted by Nazi scientists in the concentration camps of the Second World War.

As with so many moral questions, the problem is to know where to draw the line. Jesus of Nazareth was a healer. He cured diseases, and showed that God's purposes include overcoming 'those things in his creation that spoil it and that diminish the life of his children'. Clearly, where genetic manipulation is the means of healing diseases – in animals or humans – it is to be welcomed. But the dangers of it falling into the wrong hands and being used for evil ends are obvious.

The Methodist Church has supported the setting up of Ethics Committees and such bodies as the Human Fertilisation and Embryology Authority which supervise work in the genetic sciences in hospitals and laboratories to make sure that they truly serve the common good.

Basis: *Human Genetic Engineering – Good or Evil?* Dr David Hardy, Methodist Publishing House; 'Whose Life Is It Anyway?' Andrew Fox, Headway Lecture, 1998.

The Religious Society of Friends (Quakers)

According to the leaflet *Quaker Views No. 4, Genetic Engineering and Fertility Research*:

Quakers have not produced a statement about this rapidly developing area of concern but we are becoming increasingly aware of the enormous powers of modern genetic engineering techniques to change both the animal and plant kingdoms in a way that past generations could never have imagined.

While there are benefits already from using this technology, there are also great risks – for instance to the balance of nature. We notice that it is mainly people in wealthy countries who benefit from the advances in bioengineering to plant and animal species – at the expense of the people in materially-poor countries. Continuation of these technologies and their extension to human beings make it all the more important to continue to affirm our belief in 'that of God in everyone'. This means that we value all life forms, not just because they are useful to us. In fact we celebrate the great diversity amongst human beings of different races, abilities and experiences. Our *Advices* ask us to 'seek to maintain the beauty and variety of the world.'

At a personal level Quakers may encounter some of the issues involved in the area of fertility treatment. It may be difficult to think clearly about the moral issues when the situation is complicated by a deep longing for a child. Each couple will need to think carefully about several questions in coming to a decision about whether in-vitro fertilisation is right for them. For example

• What happens to unused embryos?

• Is it right to use donated sperm or eggs?

• Will the vast cost be justifiable when so many children elsewhere in the world are starving?

• Will children born from donated sperm or eggs experience the same longing that adopted children experience to find their natural parents?

While there is no statement issued by Quakers yet on this subject there is a way of thinking which involves prayerfully considering the issues on all sides.

Included in *Quaker Faith and Practice*, 29:05 was a passage which Quakers found helpful in this respect:

We recognise the enormous powers of newly developing genetic engineering techniques to change living matter with speed and scope hitherto unthinkable. Recent applications of bioengineering to plant and animal species have benefited mainly people in materially wealthy countries at the expense of the materially poor, and of global biodiversity. Continuation of these technologies and their extension to human beings highlights the need for Friends to affirm that the intrinsic value of all life forms is not restricted to their utilitarian functions, and that the richness of human diversity should never be reduced to the level of a commodity or made subject to market forces. The potential of genetic technologies for good and ill requires humility, wisdom, and loving kindness, and also the capacity to know when to stop. We Friends need to bring our own diverse gifts to help ensure that research into the application of genetic technologies do not proceed without consideration for justice, democracy, and respect for the dignity and well-being of all.

The Roman Catholic Church

The term 'bioengineering' is very broad including the genetic enhancement or modification of human, plant, and animal cells as well as the creation of new agricultural and other foodstuffs.

The biotechnological industry is fast growing. Whilst recognising the potential benefits of the application of science in this way, the Church is mindful that it must be for the service of people and not to undermine their dignity nor threaten the balance of nature. The development of super crops, for example, may have a devastating effect on traditional agricultural communities across the world and create a monopoly of distribution controlled by multinationals. The issue of how safe GM (genetically modified) food products are has been the subject of widespread debate in recent years, as well as what effect such products might have on other crops when introduced into a natural environment. The *Catechism of the Catholic Church* provides some insights into the principles underpinning a catholic approach to these issues.

The seventh commandment ['You shall not steal'] enjoins respect for the integrity of creation. Animals, like plants and inanimate beings, are by nature destined for the common good of past, present and future humanity. Use of the material, vegetable and animal resources of the universe cannot be divorced

from respect for moral imperatives. Man's dominion over inanimate and other living beings granted by the Creator is not absolute; it is limited by concern for the quality of life of his neighbour, including generations to come; it requires a religious respect for the integrity of creation (CCC §2415).

There are also applications of biotechnology for the pharmaceutical industry involving the production of insulin, growth hormones and vaccines. Once again respect for the natural world and the dignity of the human person should be the guiding principles. While the Catechism notes that 'medical and scientific experimentation on animals, if it remains within reasonable limits, is a morally acceptable practice since it contributes to caring for or saving human lives', it concludes that 'it is contrary to human dignity to cause animals to suffer or die needlessly.' (CCC §2417–8).

As regards genetic engineering on human subjects, the Church does permit some interventions by means of Somatic Cell therapy, but not Germ-line therapy techniques which would involve an impact on future generations. The majority of scientific opinion is also very cautious about the latter and generally against its development.

John Paul II in his Message for the World Day of Peace in 1990, reflecting on these matters, said this:

All attempts to interfere with man's chromosomal or genetic heritage which are not therapeutic, but tend towards the production of human beings selected according to sex or other pre-established qualities, are contrary to the personal dignity of the human being, his integrity and his identity. Creation of new transmissible characteristics in animals can be ethically acceptable if its purpose is the real good of mankind and on condition that it should not disturb the biological balance of nature.

There is, subsequently, great concern over the possibility of human cloning. The Pontifical Academy of Science issued a statement in 1997, stating that it potentially violated two fundamental human rights: 'equality' and 'non-discrimination'. Furthermore:

In the cloning process the basic relationships of the human person are perverted: filiation, consanguinity, kinship, parenthood. A woman can be the twin sister of her mother, lack a biological father and be the daughter of her grandfather. In-vitro fertilisation has already led to confusion of parentage, but cloning will mean the radical rupture of these bonds.'

Investigations aimed at creating a 'map' of the genes of the human body (The Human Genome Project) can be of benefit; but also bring with them the possibility of putting all the emphasis for human identity, uniqueness and behaviour on our DNA. Writers like Brian Appleyard warn of 'geno-centrism' in which we concentrate on finding genetic explanations for the nature of human beings at the expense of their freedom to choose as 'individuals' in response to their circumstances. In such a designer world-view what happens to concepts like normality or disability and

who decides about them? What is the relationship between the geneticists and society?

All of this points to the need for the dialogue in bioethics – called for by the Pope in *Evangelium Vitae* (EV§27) – between all people of goodwill in the search for principles which enhance the dignity of what it is to live a truly 'human' life and build-up the common good for future generations.

Added importance is given to this in the wake of recent developments in the patenting of genes by companies, for profit, and the exploitation of indigenous peoples for the unique properties contained in their blood and hair samples in what some writers call 'genopiracy' or 'genocolonialism'.

There are no contributions to this section from the Russian Orthodox Church, The Salvation Army or the United Reformed Church.

Section 13 • Environment and World Development

The Baptist Union of Great Britain

Baptist commitment to right relationships extends beyond their own churches, communities and nation. It is also vital to develop just relationships with other nations, especially those of the two-thirds world. Furthermore, humans are clearly failing to live in a right relationship with God's creation; this is an issue which must be addressed as a matter of urgency.

The environment

Baptists believe that the earth and its fullness belong to God who created it. Humanity is a part of that created order and has the God-given task of being the steward of such a beautiful and abundant resource. As steward, the human race is responsible for the maintenance of what God has made: every species, the ecological balance and so on.

A failure to acknowledge and honour the integrity of creation will lead to harm for the earth and for humans as a part of it.

World development

The difficulty with the word 'development' is that it can mean almost anything. Baptist commitment to right relationships and their opposition to all forms of oppression leads them to favour certain kinds of development and to be opposed to others.

Baptists are in favour of programmes which develop people, for example projects that enable the poor, acting together, to promote the kinds of changes that they want in their own communities or to respond to and to control those external changes which are affecting them. Good development practice is participatory; it is done by the people who will be affected, not imposed on them or done on their behalf. Development workers act as catalysts who encourage and enable the poor themselves to promote change. What poor groups and communities choose to make their priority (clean water, health programmes, housing, small industries and so on) is important but secondary to the main point, which is that the programme should be one to which they are committed and for which they regard themselves as responsible.

In addition, many Baptists believe that the economic development of poorer countries is hampered by unfair trading relationships imposed by richer, more powerful countries such as Britain. Their commitment to right relationships and to a just order means they are prepared to use such political and economic power as they may have to campaign for fairer trading arrangements and for the abandonment on the part of Western governments and banks of their right to claim interest and capital on debts owed by countries of the two-thirds world. The terms of many such debts simply increase and reinforce the differences between the industrialised countries of the West and the poorer countries of the world.

The Church of England

The biblical and theological principles which underpin the Church of England's views on issues relating to the environment and world development relate to the idea of Christian stewardship, and the human responsibility this implies. The General Synod, affirming its belief and trust in God the Father who made the world, believes that the dominion given to human beings over the natural order, is that of stewards, who have to render an account. Human beings are part of God's creation. All parts of creation are interdependent and are linked to all other parts.

The General Synod has urged the Government:

- To take all possible steps, both nationally and internationally, to establish a just and economical use of the Earth's energy resources and to minimise the impact of consequential environmental pollution;

- To take positive steps to curtail damage to flora and fauna by human activities in this country and to seek to extend such restraint elsewhere in the world;

- To consider what contribution it can make to the encouragement of the stabilising of the world's population so that human beings can live in sustainable harmony with the rest of the natural order and flourish without want.

Issues of world development relate to the existence of poverty and the inequality between the developing and the developed world. The Church sees helping the poor and fighting for justice as a Christian duty, and issues of sustainable economic development as of abiding importance. This commitment is expressed through the aid agencies and partnership with mission agencies, through the international structures of the Anglican communion, through its own studies, through continued support for One World Week and through initiatives at parish and individual level. In particular, the Church seeks to correct the systematic injustice resulting from the international debt crisis. It has welcomed partial debt-relief and has invoked the principle of 'Jubilee' (see Leviticus 25) to provide a theological rationale for providing release from unjustly imposed and unpayable debt. The General Synod endorses the aims and work of the Jubilee 2000 campaign.

The Church of Scotland

Christians have a duty to care for the environment, because 'the earth is the Lord's'. Human beings are fellow creatures with the rest of the created order, alike dependent on God. We should demonstrate a sense of respect for everything which God made.

Instead of exercising humility and prudence in our pursuit of progress, we have spoiled God's gift of creation by selfish exploitation.

Renewable resources, like the rain forests, are unable to regenerate at the rate at which they are used. Major climate change could make many parts of the earth uninhabitable for human life, or indeed for many forms of animal and plant life.

The growth in the human population threatens the balance among the species. It means that the natural resources available for human life have to be shared out among so many more people and are used up faster.

It is often a matter of Sustainability versus Development. Sustainable living should aim at improving the quality of human life, enabling communities to care for their own environment while conserving the earth's vitality. We should always be looking at development in terms of how it will affect life-styles, the environment, and the choices and opportunities it may create for the poor.

Sustainable development is development that meets the need of the present without compromising the ability of future generations to meet their own needs.

It is as much a spiritual problem as a scientific or economic problem. It is a spiritual problem because it has to do with our responsibility to each other and to the world as part of God's creation, and our realisation of our interconnectedness and inter-dependence.

It cannot be stressed too much that, both individually and collectively, we need to re-examine carefully our lifestyle and assumptions.

The Methodist Church

The environment

> The health of the environmental system is critical to all life and immensely fragile in the face of the demands of a consumerist and technologically powerful culture.

The universe as a whole is a product of God's creative and imaginative will. All its parts are interdependent. Men and women are to be stewards, not exploiters of its resources – material, animal and spiritual. Christians must support those working for conservation and the development of more appropriate, sustainable life-styles.

Basis: *Christian Faith Concerning the Environment*, Methodist Conference, 1991.

World development

In recent years countless resolutions and reports have been adopted by the Methodist Conference recognising the obligation laid upon Christians (a) to go to the relief of those in need, (b) to ensure rehabilitation after natural disasters, and (c) to assist in fundamental development – so as to enable people to become responsible for their own futures.

Throughout this period the church has pressed for the British Government to support and participate enthusiastically in multilateral and bilateral aid programmes, and to increase the proportion of the Gross National Product devoted to overseas aid. It has also pressed for the adoption of fairer conditions of trade between countries of the industrial North and those of the impoverished South as well as remission of the debt of the poorest countries.

The Russian Orthodox Church

The environment

> Your enjoyment of the world is never right
> till every morning you awake in Heaven,
> see yourself in your Father's palace,
> and look upon the skies,
> the earth and the air
> as celestial joys.

Thomas Traherne

The whole of creation is blessed by God and bears the presence of God within it. Human beings are created in the 'image of God', that is to say in the image of the Divine Son, the Second Person of the Trinity. Our calling, then, as human beings is very special. It is to be priests of creation, to offer the world back to its creator, to render the creation articulate, to transfigure the cosmos that it can articulate the 'works of the Lord' (see the Song of the Three Children[1]). In our very being we are to relate to the whole of creation.

The created world is not just a gift to us; it is a task for us. We are called in Genesis to have dominion but dominion does not mean domination. Dominion is directly related to our being created in God's image; it can only be exercised in obedience to God. Hence, the duties of man towards nature are based on the faith that God, who is the creator of nature and everything in it, loves his creation and providentially cares for it. The ecological crisis of the contemporary world cannot be solved by external measures, by any number of technological fixes. It can only be solved by a radical change of heart (*metanoia*). Orthodox theology insists that the Incarnation does not concern merely the correction of something that has gone wrong. Rather it completes God's purpose at creation. It is about the flourishing of all life. The Incarnation is about the restoration and renewal of the whole of creation. The change of heart means that we must enter into the life of God as he, through the Word, makes all things new. Voluntary self-restraint, a growing understanding of the real

---

1 This appears in some manuscripts of the Old Testament book of Daniel between verses 23 and 24 of chapter three. In modern English translations it usually appears as a separate book in the Apocrypha.

difference between want and need, a giving away of that which we do not need. This change of heart must work at many different levels in society, but the Orthodox belief is that it has to begin with ourselves. We need personally to develop the qualities of vigilance, inner clarity, mindfulness, wholeness and integrity which are implied by the traditional (but now somewhat unfashionable) virtues of chastity and sobriety.

In recent years Orthodox theologians have been at the forefront of a number of environment initiatives. A key moment was a statement made by the late ecumenical Patriarch Dimitrios on 1 September 1989, where the urgency of the situation facing us all was made very apparent:

> Man has lost the sense of sacredness of creation and acts as its arbitrary ruler and rude violator. Instead of the Eucharistic and ascetic spirit ... we observe a violation of nature for the satisfaction not of basic human needs ... but of constantly increasing desire ... But creation 'groans and labours in all its parts' ... The price of [man's] arrogance will be his self-destruction if the present situation continues.

The first day of September has always been kept as the beginning of the Orthodox liturgical year. Since 1989 it has also been kept as a day of special prayers for the whole of creation. Many conferences on environmental protection have been held in the intervening years; there have also been many youth ecology training seminars, monastic organic farming projects and so on, which have succeeded in raising the consciousness of more and more Orthodox Christians in this whole area.

Care for the environment is absolutely fundamental to an Orthodox understanding of the creation and our place in it.

> Ultimately the whole of creation is destined to become a transfigured world. The salvation of humanity necessarily involves the salvation of its natural home, the cosmos. (Report of WCC Inter-Orthodox Consultation, Sofia, 1987)

Nature is seen within the framework of spiritual illumination, a contemplation in which God speaks to men. It can never lead to a science which deposes God or a technology which leads to sin (separation of man from God).

World development

From the above it should be clear that from an Orthodox perspective the only 'development' which is ultimately real is that which transfigures the world by bringing it back to God as a sacred offering. When most people in the contemporary world think of development, they are thinking in terms of human beings having increasing control and knowledge. This may be control over political processes, control over disease, scientific knowledge of material processes and so on. Clearly within these parameters some forms of development are better than others in that some alleviate suffering whilst others cause more suffering.

From an Orthodox perspective, however, the only development which really counts brings human beings neither control nor knowledge. We cannot develop the cosmos in the way that God intends us to without that radical change of heart (*metanoia*) already referred to. With that change of heart, however, we can let go of our attempts to control and we can therefore allow God to act. Knowledge then dissolves into something much deeper, the wisdom of understanding our unique place in the cosmos.

The Religious Society of Friends (Quakers)

Quakers see the problems caused by poverty, the abuse of human rights, the destruction of the natural environment and the exploitation of both people and the earth, as intrinsically linked.

Their concern about poverty, the distribution of wealth and development stems from their shared belief that there is 'something of God in everyone' and in that respect we are all equal. Equality, justice and peace are closely linked to the Quaker peace testimony, because Quakers believe that where poverty rules, peace cannot prevail. The seeds of war lie in injustice and tyranny, as well as fear and mistrust. Quakers believe that it is wrong to let people in one part of the world starve, whilst others have plenty.

Quakers believe that the air, sea, earth, forests, animals and ourselves are all intimately connected, and that the way in which we treat all of those things reflects on ourselves and consequently on God. Quakers try to live a simple life which respects people, the earth and the gifts of the earth. Quakers believe that the destruction of the good

things we have on earth impoverishes us as well as the environment.

Quaker writings guide them in their thinking on these issues. John Woolman, an 18th century American Quaker, said, 'The produce of the earth is a gift from our gracious creator to the inhabitants and to impoverish the earth now to support outward greatness appears to be an injury to the succeeding age.' His concern was that in the pursuit of a quick accumulation of wealth, people were not addressing the human needs of the people who were then slaves, nor the needs of the earth. He proclaimed that if people abused the earth then, it would make problems for future generations. These are things which concern Quakers still.

For Quakers today, development is about justice, peace and the considerate use of the environment. They believe that everyone should have the right, the responsibility and the freedom to work towards this end. In the so called Third World – or the South – they believe that there is a conflict between the needs of the people who live there and the demands of the North which maintains its control through unfair financial and commercial practices. Quakers believe that people everywhere need to listen to and understand one another.

As a result of their beliefs, particularly the peace testimony, Quakers have several areas in which they work to help alleviate the effect of exploitation, poverty, environmental degradation, conflict and disease. The aim is also to help tackle the root causes of such problems. Quaker Peace and Service has workers in areas of conflict, where there may be possible openings for peacebuilding or mediation. Quakers have workers in the United Nations who help to support efforts made towards sustainable development and the redistribution of resources. The importance, for Quakers, is that all of these problems are linked, and the central issue is peace. For Quakers, peace goes beyond opposition to war. It leads them to seek harmony with all living things and the right relationship with the planet.

The Roman Catholic Church

The environment

In the last twenty years the Popes and the Synod of Bishops have often drawn attention to the need to care for the environment. In his most recent statement on these issues, *Sollicitudo Rei Socialis*, 1988, Pope John Paul pointed to the positive signs that humanity is being brought together, among other things by the greater realisation of what he calls 'ecological concern'.

He calls for a moral response to the whole environment based on certain definite principles.

1 The earth and all life on it is a gift from God given to us to share and develop, not to dominate and exploit.

2 Our actions have consequences for the rights of others and for the resources of the earth.

3 The goods of the earth and the beauties of nature are to be enjoyed and celebrated as well as consumed.

4 We have the responsibility to create a balanced policy between consumption and conservation.

5 We must consider the welfare of future generations in our planning for and utilisation of the earth's resources.

World development

The Church exists 'to proclaim good news to the poor [and] freedom for the oppressed'. It takes Christ's words, 'as you did it to the least of my brethren you did it to me', not just on a personal level, but also a social one.

Nine main themes can be identified in the teaching of the Church in the last fifty years. The document referring to each theme is bracketed at the end of the sentences.

1 Religion and world development
There is no separation between the religious and the secular world. It is all God's; therefore faith and justice are linked together. (*The Church in the Modern World*, Second Vatican Council)

2 The dignity of the human person
Made in the image of God, women and men have certain inalienable rights. The fundamental question to ask about social development is, 'What is happening to people?' (*Peace on Earth*)

3 Option for the poor
A preferential love should be shown to the poor who, as a consequence of their status, suffer oppression and powerlessness. Their needs and rights are given special attention in God's eyes. (*A Call to Action*)

4 Link between love and justice
Love of neighbour must express itself in working for structures which respect human dignity, protect human rights and help human development. Justice transforms structures which deny love. (*Justice in the World*)

5 Promotion of the common good
The common good means all those conditions of human living, economic, political, cultural, which make it possible for women and men to achieve the perfection of their humanity. Individual rights are always upheld within the context of promotion of the common good. (*Christianity and Social Progress*)

6 Economic justice
The economy is for all the people and the resources of the earth are to be equitably shared by all. Human work is the key to contemporary social questions. Labour takes precedence over both capital and technology in the production process. Just wages and the right of workers to organise are to be respected. (*On Human Work*)

7 Stewardship
All property has a 'social mortgage'. It is 'borrowed'. All people are to be respected and to share the earth's resources. By our work we are co-creators in the continuing development of the earth. (*On Human Work*)

8 Global solidarity
We belong to one human family and must therefore promote the development of all people everywhere. In particular, the rich nations have responsibilities towards the poor nations, and international relations must reflect justice. (*The Development of Peoples*)

9 The promotion of peace
Peace is the fruit of justice and is dependent upon right order among humans and among nations. The arms race must cease and progressive disarmament take place if the future is to be secure. In order to promote peace and the conditions of peace, an effective international authority is necessary. (*Peace on Earth*)

The Salvation Army

As people made in the image of God (Genesis 1:27), we have a responsibility to use resources of the earth in a way that ensures that people in this and future generations do not suffer from poverty or injustice. This is part of our stewardship of the earth and our love of others. In the modern world, Christian stewardship implies large scale and permanent changes in attitudes and behaviour towards God's creation, so that we begin to 'replenish the earth' (Genesis 1:28).

Responsibility was given to humanity to 'cultivate and keep' the earth (Genesis 2:15) but humanity has destroyed or is destroying much of God's creation (Isaiah 24:4–5).

God's instruction to 'subdue' the earth and 'rule' over every living thing (Genesis 1:28) cannot be interpreted as justifying exploitation. God gave his people rights and privileges, but these included duties and responsibilities. Given the finite resources of the world and its expanding population, together with the impact of industrial and rural activities, development must take into account the need to preserve the earth as an exercise in responsible stewardship.

Source: International Leaders Conference, 1992.

The United Reformed Church

Environment

The United Reformed Church General Assembly of 1998 endorsed the publication of a new pack 'Roots and Branches', and passed the following resolution:

Assembly

a recognises with thanksgiving and repentance that the care and stewardship of God's creation is an essential part of Christian discipleship;

b challenges every local church to address its own responsibilities over the next two years, using the pack 'Roots and Branches';

c in particular, instructs Church and Society, in conjunction with other committees, to develop a plan for energy audits of church premises;

d invites District Councils to consider these matters in their regular visits to churches.

The need for Christians to treat the natural order with more care and reverence has been growing in recent decades. The formula 'Justice, Peace and the Integrity of Creation' has encouraged us to emphasise concern for the created order, but never at the expense of human justice and world peace. Thus we have been developing a holistic approach which seeks to base Christian environmental concerns in scripture and the Christian tradition while welcoming the discoveries and heeding the warnings of contemporary science.

The pack 'Roots and Branches' is user-friendly, designed round the needs and experiences of different groups or interests within a local congregation. There is material for children and young people, worship leaders, fabric committees, house groups, caterers and so on – the 'branches' hopefully bearing fruit. Complementing these is material exploring the 'roots', with basic statistics, case-studies from churches, bible studies, glossary, passages from distinguished Christian writers, resource lists and so on. The plan is for a Church Meeting to work out some policies to 'green the church' and report back on how the ideas have caught on and are affecting various aspects of church life.

One particular environmental concern is global warming with its serious impact of rising sea levels and climate change. Global warming is a consequence of the release of certain gases into the atmosphere, the main contribution coming from the burning of fossil fuels (coal, oil and gas). For what is often a modest capital outlay, significant savings can be made in fuel bills. 'Greening the church' is not some extraneous or 'new age' notion but a return to fundamental beliefs about God and the creation and our stewardship as human beings.

World development

World development has had a high profile within the URC since its inception in 1972. Following a United Nations recommendation that the developed nations should spend 1% of their Gross National Product on overseas aid, the Presbyterian and Congregational Churches in England and Wales, before their union in 1972, established a World Development 1% Appeal to match the call to governments. The appeal was for 1% of annual take-home pay 'until such time as the Government of the day reaches the 1% target for overseas aid'. This self-tax was a sign of commitment to the human family and of Christian hope which refuses to be paralysed in the face of human suffering and deprivation.

In 1992 the 1% appeal was incorporated into a new world development programme, 'Commitment for Life'. As well as suggesting 1% as a financial target for giving to overseas projects and development education and campaigning in this country, 'Commitment for Life' emphasises also other ways of involvement in development issues, for example worship and bible study, consumer responsibility, speaking out on issues of world justice.

The URC regards it as essential to work alongside other churches, aid agencies and secular organisations in this field.

Wealth and poverty issues are increasing reflections of the divisions in our own society as well as on the global scale. The General Assembly has endorsed the Declaration prepared in 1990 by Church Action on Poverty, *Hearing the Cry of the Poor*, and has passed several other resolutions on these issues.

Section 14 • Peace and War

The Baptist Union of Great Britain

Peace is the condition which exists when relationships are right. This means that it is more than the absence of war. War occurs when relationships between countries or within countries break down to the point that organised groups seek to resolve their differences by means of violence. Therefore, war is a symptom of broken relationships. Since Baptists place a high value on getting relationships right, we are, like other Christians and most other people, in favour of peace and against war.

The beginnings of some branches of Baptist life in Britain were influenced by the continental Anabaptists, at the forefront of the so-called Radical Reformation. Many of these groups were known for their renunciation of violence as a means for resolving conflicts. Their influence continues to be felt in Baptist circles. Certainly, Baptists have always included conscientious objectors to violence. Even those who disagree with such a position have respect for the motives of those who adopt it.

However, it must be admitted that Baptists are divided as to whether or not war can ever be a Christian response to a breakdown in human relationships. Most Baptists believe that all possible non-violent means should be used to attempt to restore broken relations and to persuade aggressors to renounce their actions. Some of us believe that violence is sometimes justified as a last resort when all such other means have failed.

In 1984 a poll of Baptist churches taken in advance of the Baptist Assembly revealed that a majority of our denomination was opposed to British possession of nuclear weapons; so far as we are aware, no existing classical theological rationale for war can be stretched to allow for the use of nuclear, biological or chemical weapons. However, some Baptists hold that the possession of such weapons is justified as a threat and as a deterrent even if their use could not be justified. Of course, this position is coherent only if the perceived enemy does not know or does not believe that this is the basis on which the weapons are possessed. Nearly all Baptists are opposed to the first use of nuclear weapons by our nation.

In conclusion, we may say that Baptists believe that true peace exists only where relationships are right. This implies that justice is a prerequisite of peace and that any injustice is a threat to peace. In consequence, we see justice and peace as being interrelated and we see it as the role of the church to reconcile, mediate and help make relationships just and fair in order to promote and maintain a lasting peace.

The Church of England

There is a long-established tradition of pacifism in Christianity. But although Christians always pray for peace, the Church as a whole has never condemned all wars or the use of force. The Church of England is involved in ongoing debate on the ethics of peace, deterrence and war.

There are within Church tradition two main frameworks for discussing the issue, the 'Just War' theory and 'Consistent Pacifism'. The Church of England is not a consistently pacifist church, so the ethical debates on war and peace have generally been conducted within the Just War framework. In its modern form the theory of Just War has involved showing that five conditions are fulfilled:

1 The war must be a defensive response to unjust aggression;

2 There must be a realistic chance of success;

3 There must be some proportion between the costs and the post-war settlement;

4 Only military targets can be chosen;

5 The force must never be an end in itself.

Current issues of particular concern for the Church of England include the development of modern technology and weapons of mass destruction, the issue of deterrence, the proliferation of nuclear, chemical and biological weapons, the issue of responsible arms transfer and the urgency of the task of making and preserving peace.

In relation to all of these issues, the task of the Church of England is not to determine defence strategies but rather to give a moral lead to the nation. The General Synod has reaffirmed its belief that indiscriminate mass destruction in war cannot be justified in the light of Christian teaching. It has encouraged Christians to explore the moral and theological issues to enable them to make more informed and committed contributions to the making and preserving of peace and to search for ways of resolving conflicts other than by war.

The Church of Scotland

The Church of Scotland has had to struggle with the problem of how to oppose evil and aggression and how to interpret the teaching of Jesus with regard to war.

Some believe that, since freedom is a basic human right, there are times when it is necessary to use force to combat evil and to defend to weak and the powerless.

Others believe that for a nation to use weapons of whatever kind is always wrong. They believe that Jesus' teaching about love and self-sacrifice is all-important. War is so evil and destructive that it is better to suffer and even be killed than to resist or defend yourself using weapons of war.

The Church has gradually come to the view that the use of nuclear weapons would be wrong and that there should be total nuclear disarmament throughout the world. Nevertheless some still hold to the view that such weapons are necessary as deterrents.

The Church considers that the Trident missile programme and the building of large missile-carrying submarines make no strategic sense. Trident should be included in the process of an orderly international reduction of nuclear weapons It maintains that, despite its shortcomings, the nuclear Non-Proliferation Treaty (NPT), which came into force in 1970, points the world down the path of disarmament and weapons control.

Many people in the Church are deeply concerned about the international trade in arms and about the part Britain plays in that trade. Selling arms to a country for legitimate self-defence is one thing; making vast fortunes out of the misery of millions of men, women and children is another.

A case has been made for the need of a peace-making force which would be in addition to and different from a UN peace-keeping force. Part of the job of this force if established would be to set up educational structures to overcome the prejudices which lead to conflict. The Church supports the establishment of such a Civil Peace Service.

Over many centuries the Church has ministered through its Chaplains to military personnel. There are approximately thirty Church of Scotland ministers serving in HM Forces.

The Methodist Church

The Methodist Church teaches that war is contrary to the spirit, teaching and purpose of Jesus Christ. On the other hand Jesus did not condemn the Centurion (Luke 7:1–10) or even Pilate himself for being part of the military arm. Instead he reminded Pilate that he had received his authority from a greater power and remained accountable to that power (John 19:10–11).

The Christian pacifist does not necessarily condemn the use of every kind of force, but refuses to employ force unaccountably or to destroy others, for example in either personal or State violence.

The Christian non-pacifist does not justify every war, but reluctantly recognises that violence (force) may be used when authorised to defend against aggression, to rectify a breach of a boundary, or to restrain or replace a 'notorious and tyrannical' despot. The Church upholds the right of individual members conscientiously to choose between these positions, and offers pastoral support to those on both sides of the debate.

Peace *making* is the creative and positive quest for the well-being of humankind and the planet on which we all live. All Christians can seek to create a way of life deliberately designed to overcome evil with good and to promote justice for all.

The Methodist Conference has frequently condemned the possible use of all weapons of mass destruction, chemical, biological and nuclear. It has not condemned their possession for deterrent purposes. It is critical of the arms trade and in particular the trade in landmines and instruments of restraint (prison irons) and torture.

Basis: *Statement on Peace and War*, 1957 and many subsequent resolutions.

The Religious Society of Friends (Quakers)

Quakers consider the question of nuclear weapons in the context of their wider commitment to peace, which is reflected in their historic peace testimony. There is a wide range of opinion, activity and engagement on nuclear weapons issues within the Society of Friends and they aim to respect that diversity. It is not possible to give the Quaker position on nuclear weapons. This account has been written by one Quaker. By drawing on Quaker writing and consulting widely, this could be seen as a representative view, not a definitive statement.

In public statements and personal reflections, through their writings and actions, Quakers are well known for their views on peace. On this issue Friends today are heirs to a 300-year-old tradition of writing and witness against war. This tradition is known as the peace testimony and they are living it today.

It was first publicly expressed in 1660, at a time of religious ferment, civil war and persecution, in a document called *A declaration from the Harmless and Innocent People of God called Quakers* presented to Charles II. This is a short extract:

> We utterly deny all outward wars and strife and fightings with outward weapons, for any end, or under any pretence whatever. And this is our testimony to the whole world … that the spirit of Christ, which leads us into all Truth, will never move us to fight and war against any man with outward weapons, neither for the kingdom of Christ, nor for the kingdoms of this world.

Quakers believe that there is something of God – the seed of the Spirit – in all people. They believe that more can be accomplished by appealing to this capacity for love and goodness, in ourselves and in others, than can be hoped for by threatening punishment or retaliation if people act badly. This is not to ignore the existence of evil. It is to recognise that there is no effective way to combat evil with weapons which harm or kill those through whom evil is working. We must turn instead, in the words of early Friends, to the 'weapons of the Spirit', allowing God to reach out through us to that of God in those with whom we are in conflict. Spiritual weapons – love, truth-saying, nonviolence, imagination and laughter – are weapons that heal and do not destroy.

Quakers are (for the most part) pacifist; they do not join armies and in times of conscription are conscientious objectors. It is not just a negative witness – not just a refusal to use or participate in violence – but a positive commitment to peacemaking and peacebuilding. Quakers aim to 'live out their witness to peace' by considering everyday choices about the work they do, the relationships they build, what part they take in politics, what they buy and how they bring up their children. It is a matter of building relationships which are strong enough to contain conflict when it arises and enable people to deal with it in a creative way. This applies at the personal, national and international levels.

Quakers frequently review and debate the need to act on the inspiration of the peace testimony. There are numerous Quaker committees, many of which are part of the central administrative organisation of the Society in Britain, centred on Friends House in London. The Society in the UK employs over one hundred staff, many of whom work on peace issues and mediation work in other parts of the world, lobbying decision shapers on disarmament issues and providing publications to help inform and educate interested Friends.

As 'no outward weapons' are acceptable, Quakers 'utterly deny' nuclear weapons as well. Nuclear weapons, like chemical and biological warfare, are particularly horrifying because they are weapons of mass destruction. They are indiscriminate: not just soldiers are killed but civilians too; not just humans die but animal life and the environment are severely damaged; not just this generation is wiped out but life could be changed or destroyed forever. Quakers cannot accept a 'defence' based on the threat of their use.

In international relations, nuclear disarmament is one strand amongst many which Quakers wish to encourage. They protest and withdraw their co-operation from the deployment of these weapons in their name and they explore and build alternative guarantees of security, through treaties, the United Nations and international mechanisms for mediation and conflict resolution.

Nuclear weapons are a symptom of a system which accepts violence as a means of attempting to resolve conflict. Quaker experience demonstrates that conflict cannot be adequately resolved by violent means. This does not mean doing nothing and standing aside. It means finding a creative response instead. While Quakers welcome the reduction of nuclear weapons under the INF (Intermediate-range Nuclear Forces) and START (Strategic Arms Reduction Treaty) agreements in recent years, they believe that disarmament is the responsibility of all states, not just the superpowers.

Equally, work for disarmament is the responsibility of all people, not just politicians and army officers. Everyone has his or her own gifts and can use them in different ways, whether it be talking with diplomats and leaders, demonstrating on marches or outside military bases, or writing letters.

The aim of Quakers is to stop the technology of extermination by reducing armaments, leading eventually to general and complete disarmament. Most Quakers support both multilateral and unilateral disarmament efforts and see them as complementary.

It is important to remember that while many Quakers would call themselves pacifists it is not essential to be a pacifist to be a Quaker. The Quaker 'witness' on peace and the peace testimony are used as sources of spiritual and moral inspiration; they are not rules on Quaker thought or action.

The Roman Catholic Church

Nuclear issues

Since the nuclear age began there has been a developing consensus in the teaching of the Church. This can be discerned in statements from the Second Vatican Council, from the Popes and from Bishops all over the world.

Two major sources for the teaching are the Encyclical of Pope John XXIII in 1963, *Pacem in Terris* (Peace on Earth), and the Second Vatican Council's Pastoral Constitution *Gaudium et Spes*. *Pacem in Terris* laid the foundations of Catholic opposition to the arms race, especially the nuclear arms race. It called for a ban on nuclear weapons and rejection of war as a means of conflict resolution. *Gaudium et Spes* added a great deal to this, in particular the firm condemnation of 'any act of war aimed indiscriminately against large cities along with their population' as a 'crime against God and man'.

The following positions can be said to be generally agreed as Catholic teaching.

1 The only legitimate purpose of nuclear deterrence is to prevent war. It is therefore immoral to procure or deploy more weapons than are needed simply to deter a potential aggressor from starting a war. Any quest for 'superiority' is forbidden.

2 There must be no intention directly to attack whole cities or densely populated areas.

3 Because of the immediate dangers of the arms race, any policy of deterrence must itself help to promote disarmament, certainly not to make it more difficult.

4 Nuclear deterrence is not a stable means for the establishment of the security of a nation. Therefore it can be tolerated, if at all, only as a short-term expedient, providing an interlude during which political leaders must set about achieving genuine disarmament.

5 Any policy for security which includes nuclear deterrence must be compatible with, and indeed promote, human rights, co-operation and international trust on which alone a secure peace can be built.

6 Nevertheless, in current conditions 'deterrence based on balance, not as an end in itself but as a step on the way toward a progressive disarmament, may still be judged morally acceptable'.

The Salvation Army

The Salvation Army respects the right of individuals to arrive at their own decision on the question of military service, based on personal conviction.

Basing its advice on scriptural teaching concerning respect for properly constituted civil authority, the Army counsels those who object to military service to accept whatever legitimate means may be provided for alternative service.

In no circumstances does the Army regard a conscientious objector with any sense of stigma, believing that any such censure would be a negation of the love of the Lord Jesus Christ, whose power alone can enable men to learn to live together in peace.

Positional Statement 4, reissued November 1992.

The United Reformed Church

At its General Assembly in 1983 the United Reformed Church passed the following resolutions.

1 The General Assembly affirms its abhorrence of war and its commitment to peacemaking as a Christian vocation central to the Gospel of Jesus Christ, the Prince of Peace. In particular, the General Assembly calls upon all local churches and members:

   a to oppose the use of nuclear power for warlike purposes

   b to work for the removal of nuclear weapons from British territory and to oppose the deployment of Cruise missiles in the UK

   c to press for an end to the manufacture and purchase of nuclear armaments by the UK Government, and the cancellation of the proposed Trident D5 submarine programme

   d to work for an early end to the international arms race by multilateral disarmament, and as a step towards this for the UK to give up immediately its own existing nuclear armaments

   e to strengthen our Christian commitment to peace –
   i by deepening our understanding of it,
   ii by encouraging and participating in initiatives for peace at all levels,
   iii by supporting the work of the United Nations, particularly through local United Nations Association branches,
   iv and to support all peacemaking by constant prayer for peace.

2 The Assembly welcomes the publication of *The Church and the Bomb* and its discussion by the Anglican General Synod and urges study and discussion throughout the URC of the issues raised in it.

3 a The Assembly agrees that the Nuclear Weapons resolution adopted on the 25 May 1983 be sent to HM Government.

   b The Assembly further requests HM Government to urge all other nuclear weapons States to freeze all research into and development, production, acquisition, testing and deployment of all nuclear weapons and to use the period of the freeze to work for substantial reductions in nuclear weapons and their eventual elimination by all States as first steps towards more general disarmament within an internationally agreed concept of common security.

4 The Assembly instructs the Church and Society Department to co-operate with sister Churches in Britain and throughout the world in a global fellowship committed to prayer, education and action for peace and to this end instructs the Department to set up a United Reformed Church Peace Group, and calls upon local churches to explore and initiate programmes of peace education for their own members and for the communities they serve.

At its General Assembly in 1994 the United Reformed Church passed the following resolution:

   a Assembly, noting that 1995 marks the 50th anniversary of the foundation of the United Nations Organisation and of the first use of nuclear weapons, and believing that the Non-Proliferation Treaty, due for renewal in 1995, represents an important step towards the effective international control and eventual elimination of nuclear weapons, therefore calls on the Government to work for this treaty to be reaffirmed and made permanent.

   b i Assembly remains concerned over the continuing excessive dependence of British manufacturing industry on the arms trade;

   ii expresses its growing concern that revelations of possible linkages between the Aid and Trade Provision and arms deals are damaging the reputation of the British aid programme; and

   iii calls on the Government to publish applications for arms export licences so that, if necessary, there can be Parliamentary and public debate before approval is given.

There is no contribution to this section from the Russian Orthodox Church

Useful Addresses and Resources

Addresses of Contributing Churches

Contact these addresses only if you have a query not covered by this book, or if you wish to obtain more detailed resources.

The Baptist Union of Great Britain

Baptist House, PO Box 44, 129 Broadway, Didcot, Oxon, OX11 8RT, Website: http://www.baptist.org.uk

The Church of England

Church House, Great Smith Street,, London, SW1P 3NZ, Website: http://church-of-england.org.uk
Enquiries about education should be addressed to:
The National Society's RE Centre
36 Causton Street, London, SW1P 4AU.

The Church of Scotland

Department of Education, The Church of Scotland, 121 George Street, Edinburgh, EH2 4YN, Website: http://www.churchofscotland.org.uk
For further details on Animal Welfare, Bioengineering and Environment and World Development consult
The Society, Religion and Technology Project
John Knox House, 45 High Street, Edinburgh, EH1 1SR, Website: http://dspace.dial.pipex.com/srtscot/srtpage3.htm
For further details on Relationships and Family, Beginnings of Life, Homosexuality, Substance Abuse and Issues of Death consult
The Board of Social Responsibility
Charis House, 47 Milton Road East, Edinburgh, EH15 2SR.
For further details on Law and Order, Work, Money Matters and Peace and War consult
The Committee on Church and Nation
The Church of Scotland, 121 George Street, Edinburgh, EH2 4YN
For further details on Gender and Prejudice and Discrimination consult
The Board of Practice and Procedure
The Church of Scotland, 121 George Street, Edinburgh, EH2 4YN

Churches Together in Britain and Ireland

Inter-Church House, 35–41 Lower Marsh, London, SE1 7SA, Email: churchsoc@ctbi.org.uk, Website: http://www.ctbi.org.uk

The Methodist Church

25 Marylebone Road, London, NW1 5JR, Website: www.methodist.org.uk
For publications of the Methodist Church, apply to:
Methodist Publishing House
20 Ivatt Way, Peterborough, PE3 7PG, Email: sales@mph.org.uk

The Religious Society of Friends (Quakers)

Friends House, 173 Euston Road, London, NW1 2BJ, Email: qhs@quaker.org.uk, Website: http://www.quaker.org.uk

Roman Catholic Bishops' Conference Secretariat

39 Eccleston Square, London, SW1V 1PD
Website: http://www.tasc.ac.uk/cc
For publications apply to Catholic Education Service at the above address.

The Russian Orthodox Church in Great Britain and Ireland

Diocese of Sourozh, The Cathedral, 67 Ennismore Gardens, London, SW7 1NH,
Email: sourozh@sourozh.org,
Website: www.sourozh.org

The Salvation Army

Territorial Headquarters, 101 Queen Victoria Street, London, EC4P 4EP, Website: http://www.salvationarmy.org.uk

The United Reformed Church

86 Tavistock Place, London, WC1H 9RT, Website: http://www.urc.org.uk

Addresses of other Christian Organisations

CAFOD (Catholic Fund for Overseas Development)

2 Romero Close, Stockwell Road, London, SW9 9TY, Website: http://www.cafod.org.uk
Email: hqcafod@cafod.org.uk

Catholic Institute for International Relations (CIIR)

Unit 3, Canonbury Yard, 190a New North Road, Islington, London, N1 7BJ, Website: http://www.ciir.org, Email: ciir@ciir.org

Centre for Black and White Christian Partnership

Selly Oak Colleges, Bristol Road, Birmingham, B29 6LQ, Website: http://www.bham.ac.uk/cbwcp
Email: cbwcp@sellyoak.ac.uk

Christian Aid

35 Lower Marsh, Waterloo, London, SE1 7RT, Website: http://www.christian-aid.org.uk
Email: info@christian-aid.org

Christian CND

162, Holloway Road, London, N7 8DQ
Website: http://www.gn.apc.org/ccnd
Email: ccnd@gn.apc.org

Christian Ecology Link

CEL Information Officer, 20 Carlton Road, Harrogate, North Yorkshire, HG2 8DD
Website: http://www.christian-ecology.org.uk

Church Action on Poverty

Central Buildings, Oldham Street, Manchester, M1 1JT, Website: http://www.church-poverty.org.uk
Email: info-churchaction@cwcom.net

Churches Commission for Racial Justice

Churches Together in Britain and Ireland, Inter-Church House, 35–41 Lower Marsh, London, SE1 7SA, Website: http://www.ctbi.org.uk/ccrj
Email: ccrj@ctbi.org.uk

CommonWeal

41 George IV Bridge, Edinburgh, EH1 1EL.

Fellowship of Reconciliation

The Eirene Centre, Old School House, Clopton, Nr Kettering, NN14 3DZ
Website: http://www.gn.apc.org/fore
Email: fellowship@gn.apc.org

Guild of Catholic Doctors

60 Grove End road, London, NW8 9NH.

The Linacre Centre for Healthcare Ethics

60 Grove End Road, London, NW8 9NH.

MarriageCare

Clitherow House, 1 Blythe Mews, Blythe Road, London, W14 0NW.

Runnymede Trust

133 Aldersgate Street, London, EC1A 4JA
Website: http://www.runnymedetrust.org
Email: info@trt.demon.co.uk

SCIAF (Scottish Catholic International Aid Fund)

19 Park Circus, Glasgow, G3 6BE
Website: http://www.sciaf.org.uk

Tearfund

100 Church Road, Teddington, Middlesex, TW11 8QE, Website: http://www.tearfund.org
Email: enquiry@tearfund.org

Resources

Publications listed here are not necessarily currently in print. In some cases publications have been included even though they are known to be out of print because they were influential in the development of Christian thinking on a particular issue. Teachers wishing to refer to such primary sources are advised to contact the Church from which they originated.

In the resources lists below, the following symbols are used where appropriate to denote the Church from which the resource originates. Resources not originating from any particular Church are listed first within each section, after which they are listed in alphabetical order of the originating Church.

(B)	Baptist
(CE)	Church of England
(CS)	Church of Scotland
(CT)	Churches Together in Britain and Ireland
(M)	Methodist
(Q)	Religious Society of Friends (Quakers)
(RC)	Roman Catholic
(RO)	Russian Orthodox
(SA)	Salvation Army
(URC)	United Reformed Church

General

(B)   **Baptist Basics**, The Baptist Union of Great Britain, 1992.

(B)   **Radical Believers**, Paul Beasley-Murray, The Baptist Union of Great Britain, 1991.

(B)   **Living in Care and Justice, A Study Guide on Christian Ethics**, Colin Brown, The Baptist Union of Great Britain, 1995.

(CS) **Reports to the General Assembly of the Church of Scotland** may be obtained from The Principal Clerk, The Church of Scotland, 121 George Street, Edinburgh, EH2 4YN.

(M) **The Methodist Church – An Invitation**, Methodist Publishing House, 1999.

(M) **Methodist Church Statements on Social Responsibility 1946–95**, Methodist Publishing House.

(Q) **Quaker Faith and Practice, the book of Christian discipline of the Yearly Meeting of the Religious Society of Friends** (Quakers) in Britain, Britain Yearly Meeting, 1995.

(Q) **A Light that is Shining**, Harvey Gillman, Quaker Home Service, revised edition 1997..

(RC) **Catechism of the Catholic Church**, Geoffrey Chapman, 1994.

(RO) **Contemporary Moral Issues Facing the Orthodox Christian**, Stanley S Harakas, Light and Life, 1982.

(RO) **Ethics after Christendom**, Vigen Guroian, Eerdmans, 1994

(URC) **Let's Discover the United Reformed Church** – loose-leaf pack for schools and churches containing photocopiable worksheets, background notes, material for discussion and reflection, available (£11.95) from URC Bookshop, 86 Tavistock Place, London, WC1H 9RT

How the Churches Decide

(CE) **Introducing the Church of England** (a range of leaflets explaining the working and beliefs of the Church of England), ed. Steve Jenkins, Publications Unit, General Synod of the Church of England, Church House, Great Smith Street, London, SW1P 3NZ.

(Q) **Testimony and Tradition**, John Punshon, Quaker Home Service, 1990.

(RO) **The Orthodox Church**, Timothy Ware, Penguin, 1993.

(RO) **A Dictionary of Greek Orthodoxy**, Nicon D Patrinacos, Light and Life, 1984.

1 Relationships and Family

(B) **Belonging, A Resource for the Christian Family**, Anne Wilkinson-Hayes and Paul Mortimore (eds), The Baptist Union of Great Britain, 1993.

(CE) **The Book of Common Prayer**, 1662.

(CE) **The Alternative Service Book**, 1980

(CS) **The Future of the Family**, Church of Scotland Board of Social Responsibility with St Andrew Press, 1995.

(M) **Christian Preparation for Marriage**, Methodist Publishing House, 1998.

(M) **Christian Understanding of Family Life, The Single Person and Marriage**, Methodist Conference Statement, Methodist Publishing House, 1992.

(Q) **Relative Experience, A Contemporary Anthology of Quaker Family Life**, Redfern and Collins (eds), Quaker Home Service, 1994.

(RC) **Familiaris Consortio (1981): Apostolic Exhortation on the Christian Family in the Modern World**, John Paul II, Catholic Truth Society.

(RC) **Letter to Families**, John Paul II, Catholic Truth Society, 1994.

(RO) **On Marriage and Family Life**, St John Chrysostom, St Vladimir's Seminary Press, 1986.

(RO) **Marriage: An Orthodox Perspective**, John Meyendorff, St Vladimir's Seminary Press, 1980.

2 The Beginning of Life

The Morality of Abortion: Legal and Historical Perspectives, John T. Noonan (ed), Harvard University Press, 1970.

(CE) **Personal Origins**, Board for Social Responsibility, Church House Publishing, 1985.

(CS) **Pre-conceived Ideas – A Christian Perspective of IVF and Embryology**, Church of Scotland Board of Social Responsibility with St Andrew Press, 1996.

(M) **Status of the Unborn Human**, Methodist Conference Report, Methodist Publishing House, 1990

(RC) **Abortion and the Right to Live**, Catholic Archbishops of Great Britain, Catholic Truth Society, 1980.

(RC) 'Declaration on Procured Abortion (1974)' in **Vatican II Volume II: More Post-Conciliar Documents**, A Flannery (ed), Dominican Publications.

(RC) **Humanae Vitae**, Paul VI, Catholic Truth Society, 1968.

(RC) **Infertility and Assisted Conception: What You Should Know**, A Sutton, The Catholic Bishops' Joint Committee on Bio-ethical Issues, 1993.

(RC) **Instruction on Respect for Human Life in Its Origin and on the Dignity of Procreation (Donum Vitae)**, Catholic Truth Society, 1987.

(RC) **A Question of Life: Its Beginning and Transmission**, Patrick O'Mahony, Sheed & Ward, 1990.

(RO) 'Procreation and the Beginning of Life', John Breck, **St Vladimir's Theological Quarterly** 39 (3), 1995.

(RO) **Marriage, Sexuality and Celibacy: A Greek Orthodox Perspective**, Demetrios J Constantelos, Light and Life, 1975.

(RO) **An Orthodox View of Abortion**, Father John Kowalczyk, Light and Life, 1979.

(RO) **The Sacred Gift of Life: Orthodox Christianity and Bioethics**, John Breck, St Vladimir's Press, 1998

3 Gender

(M) **Report of The Commission on Human Sexuality and Related Resolutions**, Methodist Conference Statement, Methodist Publishing House, 1993.

(RC) **Love is for Life**, Irish Bishops Conference, Veritas, 1995.

(RC) **The Truth and Meaning of Human Sexuality (Guidelines for Education within the Family)**, Pontifical Council for the Family, Catholic Truth Society, 1995.

4 Homosexuality

(CE) **Issues in Human Sexuality: A Statement by the House of Bishops**, Church House Publishing, 1991.

(M) **Report of The Commission on Human Sexuality and Related Resolutions**, Methodist Conference Statement, Methodist Publishing House, 1993.

(Q) **Towards a Quaker View of Sex,** Facsimile Reprint, Quaker Home Service, 1990.

(RC) **Letter to the Bishops of the Catholic Church on the Pastoral Care of Homosexual Persons**, Catholic Truth Society, 1986.

(RC) **A Note on the Teaching of the Catholic Church concerning Homosexual People**, Cardinal Hume, 1995.

(URC) **Homosexuality: A Christian View**, United Reformed Church, 1991.

(URC) **Homosexuality and the Gospel**, United Reformed Church, 1992.

(URC) **Speaking for Ourselves**, United Reformed Church, 1995.

5 Substance Abuse

(M) **Substances of Abuse: Getting a Perspective**, Methodist Publishing House, 1995

(M) **Through a Glass Darkly**, Statement on the Attitude of the Methodist Church to Alcohol, 1987.

6 The End of Life

(B,M) **Shadows, a study pack on euthanasia**, The Baptist Union of Great Britain and Methodist Publishing House, 1994.

(CE) **On Dying Well: An Anglican Contribution to the Debate on Euthanasia**, Church House Publishing, 1975.

(CE) **Ageing**, Church House Publishing, 1990.

(CE) **Happy Birthday Anyway (Study Guide to the Report on Ageing)**, Church House Publishing, 1990.

(M)   **Euthanasia**, Methodist Conference Statement, Methodist Publishing House, 1974.

(Q)   **Facing Death**, Diana Campen, Quaker Home Service, reprint 1996.

(Q)   **Mourn Us Not: Friends' Reflections on Death and Bereavement**, Friends Fellowship of Healing, 1992.

(RC)   **Advance Directives or Living Wills**, The Guild of Catholic Doctors, St Pauls, 1998.

(RC)   **Declaration on Euthanasia**, Catholic Tru'h Society, 1980

(RC)   **Evangelium Vitae**, John Paul II, Catholic Truth Society, 1995.

7 Prejudice and Discrimination

Eye of the Storm – A Class Divided, video from Albany Video Distribution, B ittersea Studios, Thackeray Road, London SW8 3TW, Tel 0171 498 6811.

Out of the Shadows – ., History of the Black Presence in Britain 1500-1950, video from Association for Racial Justice, Talma Road, Brixton, London SW2 1AS, Tel. 0171 274 6024.

Tuesday's Documentary – Black, video from BBC Educational Training, Sales Section, BBC Enterprises Ltd, Woodlands, 80 Wood Lane, London W12 0TT, Tel. 0171 743 5588

Learning about Racism, Paul Gordon, Runnymede Trust, 1989

One Rare: A Study Pack for Churches on Racial Violence, Churches Commission for Racial Justice, 1994

(CE)   **Anglicans and Racism**, The Balsall Heath Consultation, Church House Publishing, 1986.

(CE)   **Faith in the City**, Archbishops' Commission on Urban Priority Areas, Church House Publishing, 1985.

(CE)   **Survey on Combating Racism in Dioceses**, Committee on Black Anglican Concerns, 1991

(M)   **Race into the Future**, Methodist Publishing House.

(M)   **Statement on Racial Justice**, Methodist Conference Statement, Methodist Publishing House, 1987.

(Q)   **Communicating across Cultures**, Lilamini Woolrych, Quaker Home service, 1998.

(RC)   **The Church and Racism**, Pontifical Commission, Catholic Truth Society, 1989

(URC)   **Declaration on Racism**, United Reformed Church, 1987.

8 Law and Order

Breaking Out: A Christian Critique of Criminal Justice, Adrian Speller, Collins, 1987

(CE)   **Capital Punishment** (GS Misc 177), Board for Social Responsibility, Church House Publishing, 1983

(Q)   **Six Quakers Look at Crime and Punishment**, Quaker Home Service, 2nd edn, 1985.

(Q)   **Questions of Convictions: Quakers on Crime**, Quaker Home Service, 1986

9 Work

(ES)   **Unemployment and the Future of Work**, Council of Churches for Britain and Ireland, 1997.

10 Money Matters

(URC)   **For a Rainy Day** – video pack including two booklets containing discussion outlines, bible studies, role-plays, activities, fact sheets, briefings, available (£15.95) from URC Bookshop, 86 Tavistock Place, London, WC1H 9RT

11 Animal Welfare

(CE)   **Our Responsibility for the Living Environment** (GS718), Board for Social Responsibility, Church House Publishing, 1986.

(CE)   **Animal Welfare** (GS Misc. 341), Board for Social Responsibility, Church House Publishing, 1990

(M) **Treatment of Animals**, Methodist Conference Statement, Methodist Publishing House, 1980.

(RC) **Centesimus Annus**, Pope John Paul II, 1991.

12 Bioengineering

The Human Rights, Ethical and Moral Dimensions of Health Care – 120 Practical Case Studies, European Network of Scientific Co-operation on Medicine and Human Rights, Council of Europe Publishing, 1998.

(CE) **Personal Origins**, Board for Social Responsibility, Church House Publishing, 1985.

(M) **Human Genetic Engineering – Good or Evil?** Dr David Hardy, Methodist Publishing House, 1990.

(M) **Whose Life Is It Anyway?** Andrew Fox, Headway Lecture, 1998.

(M) **Making our Genes Fit: Christian Perspectives on the New Genetics**, Methodist Publishing House, 1999.

(Q) **Inventing Heaven? Quakers Confront the Challenges of Genetic Engineering**, Quaker Home Service, 1999.

(RC) **A Brave New World?** J Scally, Veritas, 1998.

(RC) **Charter for Health Care Workers**, Pontifical Council for Assistance to Health VCare Workers, Vatican City, 1995.

(RC) **Evangelium Vitae**, John Paul II, Catholic Truth Society, 1995.

(RC) **Genetic Intervention on Human Subjects: The Report of a Working Party**, The Catholic Bishops' Joint Committee on Bioethical Issues, 1996.

(RC) **Life and Morality: Contemporary Medico-moral Issues**, D Smith, Gill and Macmillan, 1996 (also includes ecumenical perspectives).

(RC) **Medical Ethics: Sources of Catholic Teachings**, 2nd edn, K D O'Rourke and P Boyle, Georgetown University Press, 1993.

(RC) **Reflections on Cloning**, Pontifical Academy of Science, Vatican City, 1997.

(RO) **Towards a More Natural Science**, Leon R Kass, The Free Press, 1985.

(RO) **Bioethics: A Primer for Christians**, Gilbert Meilaender, Paternoster Press, 1997.

13 Environment and World Development

Christian Declaration on Nature, The Assisi Declarations, World Wide Fund for Nature, 1986.

Hearing the Cry of the Poor, Church Action on Poverty, 1990.

(CE) **Our Responsibility for the Living Environment** (GS718), Board for Social Responsibility, Church House Publishing, 1986.

(CE) **Faith in the Countryside**, Archbishops' Commission on Rural Areas, Churchman Publishing, 1990.

(CE) **Christians and the Environment** (GS Misc 367), Board for Social Responsibility, Church House Publishing, 1992

(M) **Christian Faith Concerning the Environment**, Methodist Conference Report, Methodist Publishing House, 1991.

(Q) **The Creation Was Open to Me: An Anthology of Friends' Writings on That of God in All Creation**, compiled by Anne Adams, Quaker Home Service, 1996.

(Q) **Quaker Approaches to Development**, Committee on Sharing World Resources, Quaker Peace and Service, 1988.

(RC) **Pacem in Terris: Encyclical Letter on Human Rights and Duties**, Pope John XXIII, Catholic Truth Society, 1963.

(RC) **Gaudium et Spes: Pastoral Constitution on the Church in the Modern World**, Second Vatican Council, Catholic Truth Society, 1964.

(RC) **Populorum Progressio: Encyclical Letter on Development**, Pope Paul VI, Catholic Truth Society, 1967

(RC)   ***Laborem Exercens: Encyclical Letter on Human Work***
(1981), Pope John Paul II, Translated from the Latin
by J Kirwan, Catholic Truth Society, 1984.

(RC)   ***Sollicitudo Rei Socialis***, Pope John Paul II (1988),
simplified version published as Social Concern,
Catholic Truth Society, 1990.

(RO)   ***Orthodoxy and Ecology Resource Book***, Alexander
Belopopsky and Dimitri Oikonomou, Syndesmos
Publications.

(URC) ***Roots and Branches*** – a starter pack to help churches
care for God's creation, available (£4.00) from URC
Bookshop, 86 Tavistock Place, London, WC1H 9RT

14 Peace and War

(B)   ***Towards a Theology and Practice of Peacemaking***,
Bernard Green, Baptist Peace Fellowship, 1994
(available from The Baptist Union of Great Britain).

(CE)   ***The Church and the Bomb***, Board for Social
Responsibility, Hodder, 1983.

(CE)   ***Peacemaking in a Nuclear Age***, Board for Social
Responsibility, Church House Publishing, 1988.

(M)   ***Peace and War***, Methodist Conference Statement,
Methodist Publishing House, 1957.

(Q)   ***The Claims of Conscience: Quakers and Conscientious
Objection to Taxation for Military Purposes***, Cecil
Evans, Quaker Home Service, 1996.

(Q)   ***The Quaker Peace Testimony***, Peter Brock, Sessions,
1990.

Index

This is not intended to be a comprehensive index of *every* occurrence of all significant words. Rather it aims to direct readers to *the main section* of the book where the issue is discussed (page numbers in bold type) and to any other pages outside the main section *where there is significant discussion of the issue.*

abortion, **28–36**

alcohol, 23, **47–50**

animals, 60, **77–79**, 80–83

arms trade, 93, 96

artificial insemination, 29, 34–36, 82

benefits system, 70, **73**

bioengineering, **80–84**

capital punishment, **62–67**

children, **20–37**

cloning, 77, **80–84**

conception, 25, **28–32**, 34

conscientious objectors, 92, 94, 95

contraception and contraceptives, **28–35**

crime and criminals, **62–66**, 70–71

criminal justice system, 58, 62, 63, 65

death penalty, **65–67**

debt, 72, 73, 86

divorce and remarriage, **20–27**

drugs, **47–49**

embryos and embryology, **28–36**, **81–82**

employment, 60, **68–70**, 73

environment, 75, 77, 78, 83, **85–89**, 94

equal rights and opportunities, 38, 40, 57

euthanasia, **51–56**

factory farming, 77, 78

family, **20–36**

fertilisation, **28–36**, 82, 84

gambling, **72–76**

gender, **37–40**, **42–43**

genetics, 29–30, **80–84**

homosexuality, 38, **41–46**

hospice movement, 51, 53, 55

in-vitro fertilisation, **28–36**, 82, 84

justice, 58, 60, **62–66**, 86, 88–93

living wills, 52, 54, 55

low pay, 70, 72

male and female, 37, 44

marriage, **20–27**, 28–37, 41–45

money, 70, **72–76**

National Lottery, **72–6**

nuclear weapons, **92–96**

pain control and palliative medicine, 52, 55

peace, 88–90, **92–96**

persistent vegetative state, 52, 55

poverty, 58, 63, **68–70**, **72–74**, 86, 88, 90, 91

pregnancy, **28–36**

prejudice, 38, 40, 42, **57–61**, 70

prison, **62–67**

punishment, **62–67**

race and racism, **57–61**

rape, 28–30, 32, 35–36

sanctity of human life, 28–29, 32, 51–53

sexual orientation, 38, **41–46**

sexual relationships, 21, 22, 28, 29, 31, 32, 34, 41, 46

sexuality, 22, 29, **37–46**

smoking, 47–48

stewardship, 72, 74, 77–80, 85, 86, 89, 90

suicide, 51, 54

taxation, 68, 69, 72, 73

tobacco, **47–50**

unemployment, **68–71**

war, **92–96**

women and men, **37–40**

work, **68–71**

world development, **85–91**

Printed in the United Kingdom
by Lightning Source UK Ltd.
108693UKS00001BB/125-448

9 781851 001415